M000112703

MADE WITH LOVE

A Devotional
for Handcraft Lovers

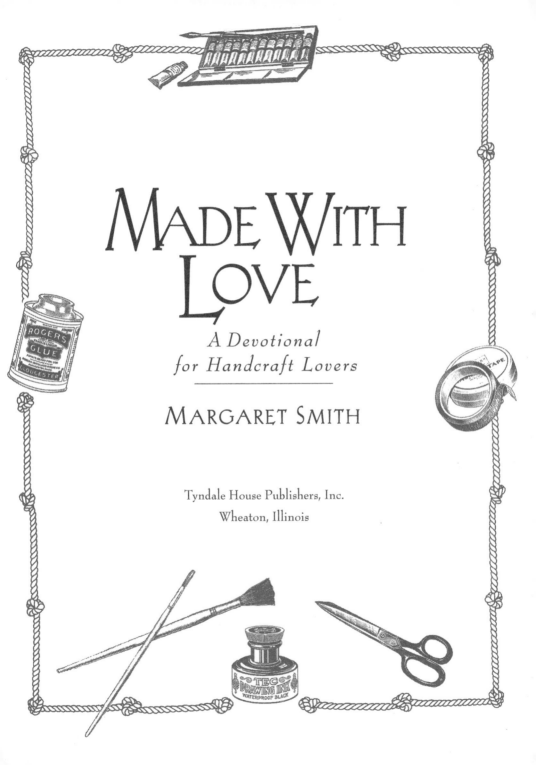

MADE WITH LOVE

A Devotional
for Handcraft Lovers

MARGARET SMITH

Tyndale House Publishers, Inc.
Wheaton, Illinois

Visit Tyndale's exciting Web site at www.tyndale.com

Copyright © 1998 by Margaret D. Smith. All rights reserved.

Cover illustration copyright © 1997 by Deborah Chabrian. All rights reserved.

Author photo copyright © 1997 by Forest Kinney. All rights reserved.

Published in association with the literary agency of Alive Communications, Inc., 1465 Kelly Johnson Blvd., Suite 320, Colorado Springs, CO 80920.

Editor: Linda Washington

Designer: Beth Sparkman

Scripture quotations marked (NLT) are taken from the *Holy Bible,* New Living Translation, copyright © 1996. Used by permission of Tyndale House Publishers, Inc., Wheaton, Illinois 60189. All rights reserved.

Scripture quotations marked (TLB) are taken from *The Living Bible* copyright © 1971. Used by permission of Tyndale House Publishers, Inc., Wheaton, Illinois 60189. All rights reserved.

Scripture quotations marked KJV are taken from the *Holy Bible,* King James Version.

Scripture quotations marked RSV are taken from the *Holy Bible,* Revised Standard Version, copyright © 1946, 1952, 1971 by the Division of Christian Education of the National Council of the Churches of Christ in the United States of America, and are used by permission. All rights reserved.

Scripture verses marked Phillips are taken from *The New Testament in Modern English* by J. B. Phillips, copyright © J. B. Phillips, 1958, 1959, 1960, 1972. All rights reserved.

Scripture verses marked TJB are taken from *The Jerusalem Bible,* copyright © 1966, 1967 and 1968 by Darton, Longman, & Todd, Ltd., and Doubleday & Company, Inc.

Library of Congress Cataloging-in-Publication Data

Smith, Margaret D., date
  Made with love : a devotional for handcraft lovers / Margaret D. Smith.
    p.   cm.
  ISBN 0-8423-1270-6 (hardcover : alk. paper)
    1. Devotional exercises. 2. Handicraft—Religious aspects—
Christianity. I. Title.
BV4832.2.S553 1998
242'.68—dc21   97-32346

Printed in the United States of America

02 01 00 99 98
7   6   5   4   3   2   1

For Mom and Dad,

who have always

encouraged me to create,

except for that one time

when I let

the vacuum cleaner

inhale Dad's fountain pen

to see if I could reverse

the flow and spray

large ink drawings

on the carpet.

CONTENTS

Introduction

Creativity can be found in whatever God the Creator has made: bright blue salamanders, unfurling jack-in-the-pulpit blooms, improbable pelicans. We can hear an echo of this busy, holy creativity in those people who follow God's inventive example. Among them are craftspeople who love to make functional objects of beauty.

Throughout my life, I've found creative people who were patient enough to demonstrate to me their particular crafts. As I look back, I find that they were also giving me insights into God's character. These insights are a significant part of this devotional.

Each of the thirty readings focuses on one person who inspired me with a craft he or she had made. In the process, incidentally, each one taught me something about the character of God. My grandfather demonstrated the humility of Jesus. A Native American weaver showed me how God cares for families through generations.

I hope you will read this devotional daily throughout the course of one month. Each time you read the Bible verses, the stories, and the thoughts that follow, you will become more aware of another characteristic of God. He is the Great Handcrafter, the one who tells the dawn to "grasp the earth by its edges" and dyes the land "like a garment." God the Craftsman in his studio lets us sit beside him like minor apprentices, watching, asking questions, until finally we are ready to work on our own imaginative handcrafts, inspiring others in turn.

"Like a quilter, God stitched you in your mother's womb. With loving thoughts he considered your whole design. He chose just the right materials, making you fine and perfect in his eyes."

My Favorite Quilt

*It was you who created my inmost self, and put
me together in my mother's womb; for all these
mysteries I thank you: for the wonder of myself,
for the wonder of your works.*

PSALM 139:13-14, TJB

When I was four, I had to share my own secret hideaway bedroom
with my baby sister, who cried a lot and got all the attention. Knowing
I needed a consolation prize, my mother gave me a family heirloom
to cover my bed. It was a hand-stitched quilt, white with reddish pink
triangles.

Before drifting off to sleep every night, I would trace the design of
those triangles. I cherished my quilt because it talked to me. Messages
were in the stitches. *I love you, I love you,* they said as they traveled their
intricate roads.

Even then my quilt was a little frayed at the edges. Maybe someone
else's child had worn out the hems a century before. Like a smelly
stuffed animal a child clings to for years, forbidding it to be washed,
the quilt certainly lost its charm for anyone else in the family. As
the years went on, reddish pink turned a softer pink, and hems fell

away. Whole edges tore off, leaving streamers in some places. Still I fingered the cotton triangles and wondered about the hands that stitched them.

A few years ago I brought my quilt out of storage. Disgusted with the way I had shredded the edges of such an heirloom, I considered cutting the usable parts into large squares. I thought I would make a few quilt pillows and finally throw out the rest.

A few days later as I was praying and listening, God said, "Pink triangles on white I love as much as you do. I hold you close. I know your every stitch. I will never discard you."

I shook my head, amazed. God cared so intimately for me that he chose the image of the quilt I loved. No one but God knew how much that quilt meant to me. I kept the quilt whole, ragged as it was. Now it's on my bed again, and I think about the hands that crafted it with love messages in every stitch.

Like a quilter, God stitched you in your mother's womb. With loving thoughts he considered your whole design. He chose just the right materials, making you fine and perfect in his eyes.

There might be days when you want to discard a part of your core self that doesn't seem beautiful anymore. "I used to think I was an artist," you might say, "but I'm not artistic, so I'm going to give up trying to make anything creative." But God sends you a message: *Don't throw out your creative drive or anything else I have given you. I designed you the way you are. I love all of you.* ✤

BUILDING ON YOUR FAITH

How do you think God sees you? Do you know you are beautiful to him just as you are? What aspect of your core self do you wish you could discard because it seems frayed at the edges? God may be asking you to cherish that worn part as well as the more beautiful parts. Remember that God loves every stitch of you.

PRAYER

Lord, you designed me to be one of a kind. Sometimes I wish I could choose which parts of myself to keep! But I see your careful craftsmanship in my fingers. I know that you love me, and I thank you.

HANDS-ON HELP

MAKE A QUILT BLOCK OF TRIANGLES. PREWASH ALL CLOTH. THEN CUT THE REMNANTS INTO EQUAL-SIDED TRIANGLES (2" EACH SIDE). ARRANGE THE TRIANGLES ON A CLOTH SQUARE IN ANY DESIGN YOU LIKE. (SCAN A QUILT BOOK FOR IDEAS.) STITCH THE FINISHED SQUARE ON THE FRONT OF A SWEATSHIRT AS YOU WOULD A PATCH. YOU MIGHT OFFER IT FOR A CHILD IN A HOMELESS SHELTER OR HOSPITAL.

YOU'LL NEED:

COTTON CLOTH REMNANTS,
   CHOSEN WITH A CHILD IN MIND
STURDY WHITE COTTON CLOTH,
   6" X 6" SQUARE
CHILD-SIZED COTTON SWEATSHIRT

A Flock
of Birdhouses

*Your gift will return to you in full and
overflowing measure, pressed down,
shaken together to make room for more,
and running over.*

LUKE 6:38, TLB

I was nine years old when I was given the rare gift of flying down
to North Carolina, all by myself, to visit Great-Aunt Sarah. She had
a way of teaching others just by giving of herself and her talents.

We sat at her piano after playing a duet, looking out at the spring
garden. In the flowering dogwoods outside her parlor window, birds
fluttered in and out of a dozen multicolored birdhouses. Every birdhouse was different. There was a Victorian one, a log cabin, a tiki hut,
and one that looked like Noah's ark.

"How did you get so many birdhouses?" I asked her.

"You know, Margaret," Aunt Sarah told me, "a long time ago, I
made a discovery. Creative inspiration is like the flu bug. And do you
know why? It's because you can't very well keep it to yourself. You just
have to pass it around. Pretty soon, before you know it, everybody's
got a real bad case of it.

6

"Now," she continued, "at the time I made this discovery I was teachin' a group of kindergarten children in Tennessee. One day I walked into class with a birdhouse I had made, and I showed it to the children.

"I didn't think my birdhouse was all that excitin'. Just a little wood box with a roof on it, a song note carved out for the hole, and a twig for the perch. Well, they were very charitable. One of the children said to me, 'I want to take that home an' show my mama!'

"Then of course, they all wanted to take home the birdhouse. So I went back home and started buildin' more birdhouses an' more birdhouses. Finally I had a flock of 'em, one for each of the children. They painted their birdhouses with all sorts of color schemes you can't imagine birds would pick for their own houses. But oh, you should have seen the proud smiles on their faces. It was as if they were each paintin' their own Sistine Chapel!

"Seven years later," she went on, "I saw how contagious the inspiration bug really was. I was retired by then and goin' through kind of a hard time, with cancer and all. Everybody at the school seemed to know when I was in or out of the hospital. Now many of these former kindergartners were still in the same school together. They were quite old by this time—about twelve, I believe.

"Before they graduated from grammar school, they decided to surprise me with their own new creations. One mornin' I woke up and walked outside in my garden, and this is what I saw!" She pointed to the birdhouses among the blossoms. "Now, that's what I call a real case of inspiration."

Just as Great-Aunt Sarah made flocks of birdhouses for children, Jesus passed around a "real case of inspiration" too. When he shared the good news of the saving love of God, the word quickly spread through towns and cities. Within a few decades, the disciples of Jesus had spread the Good News throughout the known world. The gift of Jesus' life continues to be passed on. Those who teach the Good News are in turn blessed by those they have discipled.

When we pass on our knowledge and encouragement to others, we'll be amazed at how quickly the inspiration spreads. That inspiration soon returns to us "in full and overflowing measure." ✥

BUILDING ON YOUR FAITH

Think of a time when you gave something and received much more in return. Perhaps you worked in a soup kitchen for the first time and received unexpected smiles. How did your gift inspire the person who received it? How were you in turn encouraged? What would you like to pass on to someone else?

PRAYER

Lord, thank you for the gifts of inspiration and encouragement. Help me to freely give to others what you have given me.

HANDS-ON HELP

MAKE A LOG-CABIN BIRDHOUSE WITH A CHILD. YOU CAN FIND WOOD CONSTRUCTION LOGS AT A TOY STORE. CONSTRUCT A LOG CABIN WITH A SMALL OPEN DOOR. AFTER CABIN IS BUILT, NOTE THE ARRANGEMENT OF PIECES; THEN TAKE IT APART AND CONSTRUCT AGAIN, THIS TIME USING GLUE AT JOINTS. PAINT OR STAIN TO YOUR HEART'S DELIGHT. PAINT OR STAIN A WOOD TRAY. FOR EASY CLEANING, SECURE TRAY TO BOTTOM OF CABIN WITH SCREWS. SCREW CUP HOOKS INTO THE ROOF LINE. TIE ENDS OF FISHING LINE TOGETHER; SLIP THE LINE THROUGH CUP HOOKS. HANG BIRDHOUSE FROM A TREE BRANCH NEAR YOUR WINDOW.

YOU'LL NEED:

BOX OF TOY WOODEN CONSTRUCTION LOGS
   (ONE BOX PER CABIN)
NON-WATER-SOLUBLE WOOD GLUE
THIN WOOD TRAY FOR BASE, SLIGHTLY LARGER
   THAN CABIN FOUNDATION
ENAMEL PAINTS OR WOOD STAIN WITH
   POLYURETHANE, FOR DURABILITY
BRUSHES
WOOD SCREWS (4)
CUP HOOKS (2)
FISHING LINE (36")

Fairy Treasures

The Lord shall open unto thee his good treasure.

DEUTERONOMY 28:12, KJV

For my seventh birthday, my family took me on a special trip through the markets of Chinatown in San Francisco. As we sat down at a Chinese restaurant, Dad and Mom gave me a present they had just found at one of the shops. It was a streamer ball, cinnabar red, with a gold foil seal. I had never seen one before. I was enchanted.

The streamer ball was about the size of a softball—one long crepe-paper streamer wrapped around and around itself. As I broke the seal and began to unwrap it, little treasures sprinkled out, one at a time. First there was a tiny metal spoon. Then came a clock, a plate, a lamp, and a chair, each of them unimaginably dainty, so tiny that they could easily be lost. At the very end of the streamer was a little looking glass.

I felt I was uncovering a whole treasure trove from a fairy's house. These little treasures were just the right size for me.

"I know why you gave me this present," I told my parents.

"Oh, really?" Mom smiled. "Why?"

"Because I like little presents!" I said.

"Not big presents?" Dad teased.

"I always like big presents," I agreed quickly, "but little ones are good, too, because you can keep them in your pocket. That way, they don't get lost, and you can take care of them."

The larger birthday gifts I received that day gave me only a moment of surprise, but this present offered a whole series of surprises. Each of the treasures called out to me. "Hold on to us," they seemed to say. "Watch over us; we're so small."

Like the treasure-stuffed streamer ball, each day is our own little "universe" of small presents from God. As the day unrolls, surprise love gifts appear: a phone call from a faraway friend, new flowers in the neighbor's front yard, a baby's spontaneous grin. We need to be careful not to overlook these miniature treasures. Instead we can hold onto each of them, thanking God for his meticulous care for us. ✣

What miniature treasures did you love as a child? What small treasures from God have you noticed today? Why do you think God cares about such small things? How do you think that relates to his watchfulness over the details of your own life?

PRAYER

Lord, Giver of good treasures, thank you for giving me little signs of love today. I feel happier, knowing you are watching over me with such care.

HANDS-ON HELP

MAKE A STREAMER GIFT BALL. UNROLL SEVERAL INCHES OF THE CREPE PAPER. BEGIN TAPING GIFTS AT INTERVALS ALONG STREAMER. AS YOU DO THIS, REWRAP THE STREAMER INTO A BALL SHAPE, AS YOU WOULD A BALL OF YARN. TRY TO KEEP BALL AS ROUND AS POSSIBLE. SEAL THE LOOSE END WITH A GOLD SEAL.

YOU'LL NEED:

ROLL OF CREPE PAPER, ANY COLOR, FROM PARTY-GOODS STORE

MINIATURE GIFTS (TINY GAME PIECES, DOLLHOUSE FURNISHINGS, GUM-BALL PRIZES)

TRANSPARENT TAPE

SELF-ADHESIVE, GOLD-FOIL SEAL

ROOM TO THINK

Presents from the Sea

*So don't be afraid. . . . For it gives your Father
great happiness to give you the Kingdom.*

LUKE 12:32, TLB

My friend Janet used to give me presents from the sea. We
spent summers neighboring one another on the northern coast
of California.

One August week when we were twelve, Janet kept coming up from
the beach with gifts for me. Once the gift was a branch of gray driftwood shaped like a seal. Another day she appeared with a pebble the
size of a garden pea. It was white with a black ring around it. "It's a
wishing stone," Janet explained. "You throw it in the water. But first
you have to make a wish."

There were more gifts that week: a fishbone, a silver fork—tarnished
but valuable—and a shell shaped like a trumpet. I kept all these things,
treasuring them in my cedar box under the bed.

One day Janet came to the door and asked for everything back.
"How come?" I asked.

"I just need them, OK?" she replied.

14

So I gave back everything Janet had given me from the ocean. After she left, I went upstairs and cried on the bed.

Janet stayed away for a whole week. At the end of August, while I was packing to leave for the summer, Janet showed up at the door.

"What do you want?" I asked.

"I just wanted to give you your going-away present," she said.

"Keep it," I said. "You'll probably just want it back next summer."

"Naw. You can keep it this time." Janet handed me the present—a set of wind chimes from the sea. From the seal-shaped driftwood branch hung ornaments of every kind: the wishing stone, the shell, the fishbone, the silver fork. They all clattered together in the breeze. All the gifts were there again, suspended from new fishing line, attached with new fishhooks.

"Come upstairs," I told her. "I want you to help me hang it in my room." We hung it in the window facing the ocean. "Wait, one more thing," I said. In my father's tackle box we found some more fishing line. We tied one end of the line to the wind chimes, slipped it through the hardware of the ceiling light, and sat on my bed. Then we took turns pulling on it to make the whole collection of gifts clatter and spin. When we closed our eyes, it sounded like pebbles on the beach when the waves come in.

God likes to give presents, even more than my good friend Janet. It gives God "great happiness" to give us the Kingdom (Luke 12:32, TLB). As a great love gift, he sent us his own Son, Jesus. We are given people to love, music to share, and warm sunny days to enjoy. Some gifts are ours only for a short while: someone dies, our health fails, or a friend moves away. It's difficult to hand back to God those things we thought were ours to keep.

When we lose a friend or become ill, we can easily doubt God's good intentions in the giving of those gifts. If we could trust God's friendship, placing each separate gift back in his hands, we might soon find him bringing them back to us, whole. ✢

BUILDING ON YOUR FAITH

What gifts has God given you? Are there gifts that God has given you that you're afraid he will take away? If so, think back to a time when that happened. How did you feel at first? How were you comforted?

PRAYER

Father, thank you for the gifts that you have given me over the years. Some gifts are hard to give back to you because I love them so much. But I'm willing to do what you ask of me. Help me believe that you love to give good gifts to your children.

Hands-On Help

Make a set of wind chimes out of found treasures such as seashells, beads, or trinkets from a secondhand store. Screw a cup hook into the ceiling. You can suspend your project from this while working. Cut off six feet of fishing line; reserve the rest. Make a knotted loop on one end of the fishing line; hang the loop from the cup hook. Tie other end of line to the center of stick. Use varying lengths of reserved fishing line to attach objects of equal weight to the stick. (Hint: First hang one object in the center, then work toward the center from both ends of the stick.) To hang objects without holes (like wishing stones), wrap silver-colored wire around object as if wrapping ribbon around a present, then loop fishing line through wire.

You'll Need:

Cup hook
A set of objects that make noise
   when rattled together
Fishing line (20')
Silver-colored wire
Peeled stick or
   driftwood stick

A Pinch-Pot Problem

> *Don't let the world around you squeeze you into
> its own mould, but let God re-make you so that
> your whole attitude of mind is changed.*

ROMANS 12:2, PHILLIPS

When I was a Girl Scout, I could never figure out how to fit in with the other Girl Scouts. When they wore barrettes in their hair, they looked cool. When I wore barrettes, I looked childish. "Just be yourself," my mom counseled me again and again.

"I'm trying to be myself," I countered, "but that's what's getting me into trouble."

At one meeting, our troop leader taught us how to make small pots from clay. Behind her back we called her "Miss Of Course" for reasons that will become obvious.

"Now, of course," she began, "there are two ways you can do this. You can make what's called a pinch pot, or you can form the clay around a drinking glass. The pinch pot's a little harder, of course, but it comes out looking quite unique."

Hmm, I thought. *I like unique things. I'll try the pinch-pot method.*

All the girls huddled together and decided what they were going to do.

Then each one set to work on the easy choice, forming her clay pot around a glass. I sat apart from them, carefully pinching mine. By the end of the hour, I was nervous. Everyone else's pot was perfectly shaped, with strong sides and a solid bottom. Mine looked like it had been squeezed through a printing press.

"Now," instructed Miss Of Course, "I want you all to put your name on your pot so I can tell whose they are." When she came to mine, she said with a loud voice, "Oh, Margaret, of course I can tell yours apart from the others!"

The other girls laughed at this. I hid my face in shame.

If only I had read Isak Dinesen's "The Deluge at Norderney," I could have recited this great passage to the other Girl Scouts:

> Be not afraid of absurdity; do not shrink from the fantastic.
> Within the dilemma, choose the most unheard of, the most
> dangerous solution. Be brave, be brave!

But such was not the case. When it was time to go, I left my pinch pot on the table, hoping the janitor would find it and throw it out. But that's not what happened. Later that week, Miss Of Course made a special trip to my home, explaining the story to my mom, who came to my room to ask why I wasn't proud of my pot.

"Because the other ones were so perfect!" I whined.

"But this one is beautiful to me," she said. "It has your name on it."

"Do you want it?" I asked.

"I'd love to keep it forever," Mom said. And she always has. Of course.

Like a potter who forms each bowl by hand, God created each of us in a remarkable way. Each of us has a unique set of talents and gifts.

As Paul writes in Romans 12:2 (Phillips), "Don't let the world around you squeeze you into its own mould." We don't have to conform to the world's standards, where people are expected to act like copies from a mold. Instead, we can be transformed! How? "[By changing our] whole attitude of mind," Paul writes in the same verse. This translates to a renewed mind. All of us can try to express our own God-given creativity in our everyday lives, encompassed in our smiles, our personalities, and the way we share our talents with others. When we do this, we can know that Christ is expressing himself through us. ❖

BUILDING ON YOUR FAITH

How does God help you express your originality? How do you respond when others belittle that originality by calling it "strange" or "different"? What kind of mold do you find yourself being squeezed into? How can you avoid being conformed to the world's "mold"? What does it mean to be "transformed" in your way of thinking?

PRAYER

Lord, as Isaiah prayed,
"Yahweh, you are our Father;
we the clay, you the potter, we
are all the work of your hand"

(Isaiah 64:8, TJB). Help me to
conform to your standards rather
than the world's.

HANDS-ON HELP

MAKE A PINCH POT. ON A TABLE, ROLL CLAY INTO BALL. MAKE A BASE FOR THE POT BY FLATTENING THE BOTTOM OF BALL SLIGHTLY. WITH THUMB, DIG INTO THE TOP OF BALL AND SHAPE POT BY PINCHING AROUND SIDES. WHEN CLAY HARDENS, PAINT AS DESIRED. USE MORE WATER WITH PAINTS FOR A TRANSPARENT LOOK OR LESS WATER FOR AN OPAQUE EFFECT.

YOU'LL NEED:

SELF-HARDENING CLAY
ACRYLIC PAINTS AND
BRUSHES

A Discarded Shard

> *The stone rejected by the builders has proved to be the keystone.*

1 PETER 2:7, TJB

A clay artist named Tatiana lived in a beach cabin on stilts outside the town of Petersburg, Alaska. Tatiana made ceramic wall art for state buildings. One piece stretched seventeen feet along an airport wall in Fairbanks. It was a fragmented view of clouds, the kind you might see through an airplane window.

Whenever Tatiana hated what she had made, she'd throw it out her studio window onto the rock beach, hoping the tides would accept what she could not.

Every morning, my friend Heidi would walk among the iceberg bits that washed ashore from the glacier across the strait and comb the beach in front of her Aunt Tatiana's studio, picking up what she couldn't bear to let the tides take away. I can imagine Heidi standing outside the studio window, waiting for more art to come flying down.

One year for my birthday, Heidi gave me a clay shard that she'd found on the beach. It was half a face, a broken life mask, with most

22

of the elements of a Greek tragedy mask contained in it. The half mask fit my face perfectly, and I set it on the shelf over my writing desk. At night we watched one another. Then I moved, all the way across the country, and I never saw my "broken half" again. One of the movers had thrown it away, probably mistaking it for rubbish.

The other day I was thinking about Tatiana and Heidi and the clay shard that was twice thrown out. What was useless to Tatiana was precious to me. I loved that fragile face.

Jesus was cast out like the clay shard. On the day of his crucifixion, bystanders derided Jesus, seeing him as broken and worthless. But to God, he was the most precious thing of all, the "keystone" of our faith. In the same way, you are a treasure to God. He loves and values you. Though you may feel broken at times, he sees you as precious. ❖

BUILDING ON YOUR FAITH

Have you ever felt crushed and broken, like a discarded piece of pottery? What were the circumstances? If you're feeling like that right now, what can you do to remind yourself that God loves and values you?

PRAYER

Lord, at times we have felt like shards of pottery broken on the beach. You tell us that we are precious to you. Thank you for picking us up, Lord, and finding a special place for us in your home.

23

HANDS-ON HELP

IF YOU DON'T HAPPEN TO HAVE AN ANIMAL SCULPTURE IN YOUR
GARDEN AT HOME, FIND ONE IN YOUR NEIGHBORHOOD PLAY-
GROUND, PARK, OR ZOO. PRESS ENOUGH CLAY OVER ANIMAL'S
FACE TO COVER IT COMPLETELY. SPREAD CLAY UP TO THE EARS
AND JAWLINE. BRING OUT FEATURES OF ANIMAL'S FACE BY PRESS-
ING FIRMLY BUT GENTLY ALL AROUND. LIFT OFF CLAY WHILE IT'S
STILL MALLEABLE. IF YOU WISH TO HANG IT UP LATER, USE A
PENCIL TO PUNCH A HOLE NEAR THE TOP (OR ONE ON EACH SIDE)
OF THE FACE; SET ASIDE. CLEAN OFF THE ORIGINAL SCULPTURE
WITH RUBBING ALCOHOL AND CLOTH. ALLOW YOUR CLAY MASK
TO HARDEN COMPLETELY. YOU CAN LEAVE THE MASK ALONE OR
PAINT IT FOR A FINISHED EFFECT. IT CAN BECOME A FOLK-ART
PIECE FOR THE WALL.

YOU'LL NEED:

ONE-POUND PACKAGE OF SELF-HARDENING CLAY,
   NEUTRAL COLOR (FROM ART-SUPPLY STORE)
OUTDOOR ANIMAL SCULPTURE (METAL,
   STONE, OR OTHER NONPOROUS
   MATERIAL)
RUBBING ALCOHOL
SOFT CLOTH
PENCIL
ACRYLIC PAINTS AND BRUSHES

ROOM TO THINK

Daddy Mac and One-Hand Crochet

Live in harmony with one another; do not be haughty, but associate with the lowly; never be conceited.

ROMANS 12:16, RSV

My grandfather, whom I called "Daddy Mac," was an essential part of our family. Everyone was attracted to him. Whenever he was in a room, people would gather around him to listen to him. He was like a fire in a hearth that people watch and are warmed by. Daddy Mac was humble, though quite accomplished, and unfailingly cheerful in conversation, though quite deaf.

When I was twelve, my family went to visit his home in Palm Springs. We sat wherever he was: at the long dining table, by the pool, or in the den—my favorite room, a place with old wooden horses and Oriental rugs.

I stood back, listening and watching, practicing my new one-hand crochet method on two long strings of purple yarn. All week I thought I was invisible, free to come and go through the rooms like a ghost.

They might not need me, but they might.
I'll let my head be just in sight.
A smile as small as mine might be
Precisely their necessity.
                              —*Emily Dickinson*

But one evening when the family was gathered in the den, Daddy Mac asked me to come over to his leather chair. The conversation in the room stopped. Even the ice in everyone's iced tea stopped clinking. "Now, Mah-gret," Daddy Mac began in his old North Carolina drawl, "would you tell me what that master- piece is?"

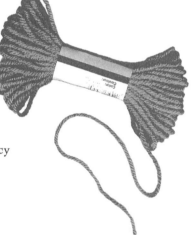

I giggled. "It's *not* a masterpiece," I said softly. Sometimes I had to shout, but sometimes he could understand everything when I whispered.

"It's not?" He sounded amazed. "Well, it certainly is to me. What do you call that fancy fingerwork you do?"

"One-hand crochet. It's pretty easy."

"It's what?"

"IT'S PRETTY EASY!"

This made everyone laugh, which was not my intention at all. Not one little bit. "Well, then," he said to me, "I think I used to be a surgeon. Let's see if you can teach an old doctor new tricks."

So I sat on the arm of Daddy Mac's chair and taught him the one-hand crochet method. "It's just a chain of slipknots," I explained.

After a few minutes he got the hang of it. I thought that once the joke was over, he would pat my back and tell me to run along. But as the buzz of adult conversation wound around us again, he whispered hoarsely in my ear, "Could I hold the yarn for you, so you can make that chain of slipknots all the way to China if you want to?"

"I like being here, instead," I said. He winked and understood.

Like my grandfather, Jesus liked to "associate with the lowly" throughout his life on earth. Just as Daddy Mac called me over to his chair, Jesus called to those who stayed on the outskirts, too insignificant to be noticed by anyone else. God is calling to you like that. He knows who you are and welcomes you to sit beside him. ✛

BUILDING ON YOUR FAITH

Was there a time when you felt invisible until a very significant person drew you into conversation? God calls to you like that during these quiet times. In a happy whisper God says, "Come sit here by me for a while. I want to spend some time with you." How will you respond to an invitation like that?

PRAYER

God, you always call to me when I feel like an outsider. You invite me into the warm circle of your presence. Let me come to you like a child to her grandfather, snuggling and sharing secrets.

HANDS-ON HELP

WITH A FRIEND, MAKE A BRACELET FOR YOURSELVES. THIS IS EASIER TO DO BY SITTING AND FACING ONE ANOTHER. FIRST, MAKE A SLIPKNOT ABOUT 6" FROM ONE END OF THE YARN. HAVE YOUR PARTNER HOLD ONTO THAT END WHILE YOU LET THE OTHER END REST IN YOUR LAP.

WITH ONE HAND, LOOSELY HOLD THE YARN A FEW INCHES BELOW THE SLIPKNOT. WITH YOUR OTHER HAND, REACH THROUGH THE LOOP IN THE SLIP KNOT AND PINCH A FEW INCHES OF YARN WITH YOUR THUMB AND MIDDLE FINGER; PULL THAT YARN THROUGH THE HOLE AND TIGHTEN THE FIRST LOOP UNTIL IT BECOMES A LOOSE KNOT. REACH THROUGH THE SECOND LOOP (THE ONE YOU JUST FORMED) AND PINCH A FEW INCHES OF YARN; PULL THROUGH AND TIGHTEN SECOND LOOP. REPEAT AS LONG AS NEEDED TO WRAP IT AROUND YOUR PARTNER'S WRIST. LEAVE 6" EXTRA YARN FOR TYING IT OFF. CUT OFF THE END OF THE YARN AND SLIP THAT END THROUGH THE FINAL LOOP; TIGHTEN. SNIP ENDS.

YOU'LL NEED:

TWO COLORS OF FINE YARN, ABOUT 24" EACH
A PARTNER

cat's paw   double sheet bend   slip knot

29

A Persistent Apprentice

Have this mind among yourselves, which is yours in Christ Jesus, who . . . emptied himself, taking the form of a servant, being born in the likeness of men.

PHILIPPIANS 2:5-7, RSV

Recently my friend Julia told me this story.

In high school, I had a boyfriend, Chet, who was a full-blooded Yupik Eskimo. He was born in a remote village in Alaska, miles and miles from the little town of Kalskag, where we were both going to a boarding school. At the time, I was one of only a handful of non-Yupiks in town. As a blonde newcomer from Seattle, I was finding it hard to fit into the culture.

One day the Yupik women in Kalskag invited me to come to their centuries-old sewing circle. At my first meeting, they tried to teach me how to sew animal skins to make clothing. But I was interested in Chet, not sewing!

Later that day, I told Chet, "I just want to go ice fishing with you."

"I want you to go, too," Chet told me, "but you know that's not traditional. You would have to be Yupik so I could marry you, and then we could go. But we can't get married because our cultures are so different. The leaders in town would never allow us to go on an ice-fishing expedition."

"How do we know they won't allow it?" I asked. "Let's go ask the leaders. Please translate for me, because I can't get through the language barrier." He agreed to try.

It took a few months of polite negotiation. Eventually Chet and I wore down the resistance of the town leaders. One of the elders who knew where the most fish were agreed to take us ice fishing. He would be our chaperone. But for a while, I had to be content with the skin sewing.

During the months I was forced to stay in Kalskag, I couldn't stop thinking of Chet. I wanted to make a present for him, something he could use when he went ice fishing. First, I borrowed some shoes from him, so I could trace boot soles just the right size. Then I bought a beaver pelt. That's a sign of high status for the person who wears it.

The women showed me how to sew the skin so the beaver fur would be inside the boots to warm Chet's feet. We sewed with special three-sided, leather-sewing needles. For thread we used, of all things, dental floss! I cut out diamonds of calfskin and sewed them as decoration around the tops.

"Mukluks." Chet smiled when I presented them to him. "No one ever gave me these before."

"Really?" I asked. "You're kidding. Why not?"

"My mom and my grandma stay in their village," he explained. "It's too far to come to the Kalskag sewing group. So they can't remember how to make them." He traced the diamond designs around the top of each mukluk. "I always wanted a pair."

"Does this make me a Yupik?" I teased him.

He nodded.

"Good," I said. "I'm going ice fishing with you."

Like my friend who learned the Yupik tradition of making mukluks, Jesus worked for a long time as an apprentice in a craft. In Nazareth he learned carpentry from Joseph. We can imagine that the painstaking labor and the skills he learned were good preparation for his later ministry. But like my friend, he had to be patient, to wait for his time to go out and do what his heart was telling him to do.

As we persevere through hard "apprenticeship" times, we can be more patient if we know that God is preparing us for something good. ✤

BUILDING ON YOUR FAITH

What kind of apprenticeship, or learning experience, are you going through right now in your life? Is it related to something you really want to do, or does it seem as if God is teaching you something completely unrelated? God honors our persistence in the lessons he sends our way, even when we can't see his larger purpose.

PRAYER

My Creator, even your Son had to become a patient servant and learn from humans. When I am listening to others today, remind me to "have this mind" of Christ and humbly learn from them.

Hands-On Help

Make a pair of mukluks for a doll. Mukluks are a type of boot with soft leather soles. Keep in mind that the fur will go on the inside of the mukluks. With a charcoal pencil, outline the soles of your doll's boots on tracing paper, adding 1/4" all around. Transfer the tracing onto the back of the pelt. Cut out the soles from the pelt. Repeat with all parts of doll's boots. (You can also use a pattern for a baby's booties.) Sew the parts together with needle and dental floss. Embroider a design or sew small beads at the top of each mukluk, if desired.

You'll Need:

A child's large doll with boots
Rabbit pelt or fake fur
  (check craft store)
Charcoal pencil
  (art-supply store)
Tracing paper
Waxed dental floss
Three-sided leather-
  sewing needle
Small colorful beads
  and embroidery thread (optional)

Yarns to Dye For

We work hard with our own hands.

1 CORINTHIANS 4:12, NIV

One morning in Juneau, our weaving class stood in the kitchen of the teacher, Carol, a crusty Alaskan who liked to do everything from scratch. She not only collected her own wool from sheep in the pastures for her museum-quality weavings, but she also dyed the yarn from plants she collected in the mountains. "Today you're going to learn to dye," she said.

Everyone was excited but me. "I'm too young to dye," I teased.

Carol fixed me with a grim smile. "You'll get the hang of it," she said. Soaking wool in boiling dye pots, she told us how to figure how many pounds of yarn could simmer for about an hour in natural dyes. "All you need to know," she said, wiping her face on her apron, "is that an hour isn't a holy time to dye." She looked around at our bewildered faces. "What I mean is," she explained, "dyeing is not an exact science."

One student asked seriously, "Does everything dye well?"

Carol winked as she continued the pun. "All things natural dye. Some hold their color, some dissolve. The more aroma a plant has, the brighter its dye will be. Marigold, spruce root, and blueberry dye very well." We braided the yarns together: yellow, green, indigo. My hands looked like a child's paintbox. I tried to rub the dyes off my fingers. But Carol admonished me, "Don't be afraid to stain your hands."

Clapping a lid on an overzealous dye pot, Carol groaned, "The instructions for dyeing should be 'Cook till it boils over; then turn it down!'"

That morning Carol taught me how to take life directly from the source, with wit. And how to dye: don't be afraid to stain your hands.

Like a weaving student afraid to stain her hands, I'm often afraid to "get my hands dirty." I try to avoid circumstances that might be too messy. Sometimes I'm more interested in "keeping my hands clean" than working hard, whether the work involves dyeing yarn, working in a soup kitchen for homeless people, or wrapping my arms around an AIDS victim. Yet God loves to work and teach in these creative situations. If I resist being stained, I resist learning some wonderful things God wants to teach me. ✤

BUILDING ON YOUR FAITH

What are some situations that you would describe as "messy" or uncomfortable for you? What happens when you try to avoid those situations? What happens when you decide to stop resisting and "get your hands dirty"? What is God teaching you during those times?

PRAYER

God, you have created the whole world, both the beautiful and the messy. And you have created me to participate in life, to stain my hands when necessary. Teach me how to "get my hands dirty" in a creative situation today.

HANDS-ON HELP

WITHOUT CUTTING IT, DYE A SKEIN OF WOOL THREE DIFFERENT COLORS. FOLLOW DIRECTIONS ON DYE BOX TO CREATE THREE DYE POTS. THREAD ONE END (ROUGHLY 1/3) OF THE SKEIN OF YARN THROUGH A WOODEN SLOTTED SPOON. PLACE THE SPOON ACROSS THE TOP OF THE FIRST DYE POT AND LET THE YARN SOAK IN THE DYE. KEEP THE REST OF THE SKEIN OUT OF THE SOLUTION. AFTER A WHILE, REMOVE AND ALLOW TO DRY. DO THE SAME FOR THE OPPO-SITE END (ROUGHLY 1/3) OF THE SKEIN IN ANOTHER DYE POT. FOR THE THIRD COLOR, THREAD BOTH ENDS THROUGH THE SPOON AND ALLOW CENTER OF SKEIN TO HANG INTO THE LAST DYE POT.

TO DYE WOOL WITH A NATURAL DYE, YOU WILL NEED A MORDANT (A FIXATIVE) TO BIND THE DYE TO THE YARN. FOR SPECIFIC INFOR-MATION AND DYE RECIPES, REFER TO A CRAFT BOOK ON NATURAL DYES.

YOU'LL NEED:

A SKEIN OF NATURAL, UNDYED WOOL
   (FROM A YARN STORE OR A SHEEP FARM)
3 BOXES OF RIT® DYE (GREEN, YELLOW,
   AND BLUE, OR 3 OTHER COLORS YOU CHOOSE)
3 POTS
WOODEN SLOTTED SPOON

ROOM TO THINK

One Woman's Cabin Is Another's Castle

*Jesus looked intently at [the fisherman] for a
moment and then said, "You are Simon, John's
son—but you shall be called Peter, the rock!"*

JOHN 1:42, TLB

Sandra lived a true Alaskan life all by herself in a remote island
cabin, where a creek moved down from the mountains, meeting a wide
channel in a calm, green eddy. I lived across the channel from her in the
town of Petersburg. When I first met Sandra on the Petersburg Harbor
dock, it was late fall. She had just docked her skiff and was coming into
town for a month's supply of groceries.

Although it was a chance meeting, we fell easily into conversation—
as Alaskans do—about projects that we needed to finish before the long
winter set in. She was eager to show me her big craft project: the aban-
doned cabin she had recently found and claimed. "You've got to see it,"
she said, waving vaguely toward one of the smaller islands. "It's so
fantastic. I've finally found the home I always wanted. And it's right
across from here."

"How would I know which cabin is yours?" I asked.

"You can't miss it," she told me. "There's a barge half submerged in

38

mud on the beach, right in front of the place. And besides, there aren't any other houses on that island."

I went in a skiff to the cabin, finding it less desirable than the palace Sandra had described. It was what real estate agents call "a handy person's dream." Black tar paper covered the exterior, except where it peeled back to reveal bare plywood. The front screen door creaked and rattled as Sandra stepped outside. "Glad to see someone!" she said. "It's been days since the last visitor."

Sandra took me inside, where one dark, musty room served as a combination kitchen and living room. Pointing out the possibilities, she mused, "I could put a sink in this corner, with running water, but not in the winter, of course. Too icy to come through the pipes then. I'm going to build a bench here, cover it with cushions, and put a log table in the center."

"How do you make a log table?" I had to ask.

She looked at me curiously, as though I had just asked how to make cold cereal. "You find a log and you set it upright," she said. "Come upstairs."

She led me up the ladder to her loft, which was crammed with books and an odd assortment of furnishings. Somehow an old iron bed had fit between the eaves. She said, "Now for a closet. Here, you think? I could move this bookshelf"—she pointed to a stack of apple crates—"squeeze one in here and still have room for a landing. How do you like the window I just put in? Found it in the woods."

"Impressive," I said. "Sandra, I came to ask if you could come to town to have supper with us."

"No," she said. "I can't. I've got the inspiration for these projects, and I can't just go and leave them. Besides, there's a nice log along the beach I want to catch for my log table before the tide comes in and takes it away."

I nodded, understanding. Not at all eager to leave that wild place but knowing how anxious she was to finish her great craft project before winter, I waved good-bye to her, guiding the skiff across the channel, back toward my own potential palace.

Sandra chose to see the potentials, rather than the limitations, of her cabin "palace." Jesus also chooses to look past our limitations to see our potential. He called an unruly fisherman to be one of his closest friends, nicknaming him "the Rock." At first unsteady, Peter took years to grow into that name. But Jesus saw him as he would become—a strong pillar of the New Testament church. "A pile of rocks ceases to be a rock pile," said Antoine de Saint-Exupéry, "when somebody contemplates it with the idea of a cathedral in mind." ✤

As you were growing up, how did someone express the potential he or she saw in you? How did you feel when that happened? What do you do to express the potential you see in others? What do you do to show people that they matter, both to you and to God?

PRAYER

God of the outcast, thank you for seeing potential in me. Thank you for showing me that you already see me complete and beautiful in your eyes.

HANDS-ON HELP

MAKE A LOG TABLE FOR A RUSTIC TOUCH. FOR A COFFEE TABLE, END TABLE, OR BEDSIDE TABLE, YOU'LL NEED TO FIND A GOOD-SIZED LOG. A GOOD CHOICE OF WOOD IS MAPLE, WHICH IS STRONG, EASY TO PEEL, AND LIGHT IN COLOR. PEEL BARK. IF LOG IS DAMP UNDERNEATH THE BARK, DRY COMPLETELY WITH HAIR DRYER. SAND, THEN APPLY THREE OR FOUR COATS OF POLYURETHANE.

YOU'LL NEED:

DRY LOG, LEVEL ON BOTH
    ENDS
SANDPAPER
SATIN-FINISH POLYURETHANE
    AND BRUSH

41

A Rose in
Stained Glass

*God does not see as [people see]; [people look]
at appearances but Yahweh looks at the heart.*

1 SAMUEL 16:7, TJB

I've always known my friend James, an insurance agent, to be a practical, down-to-earth fellow. So, naturally, I was surprised when he told me
of his greatest joy—making stained-glass gifts.

"First," he explained, "I bought a book called *Beginning Stained Glass.*
From there I learned how to make basic designs. You know—squares,
rectangles, triangles, things like that."

"Then," he went on, "I started making progress. One year for Christmas I made everyone in my family a Tiffany lamp. For every lamp I used
the favorite room colors of each family member."

I was stunned. *Wow. You mean, you cared enough to match each of their
interior design schemes?* James continued, unaware of my surprised
thoughts. "At one point, about fifteen years ago," he said, "we had a craft
sale at the insurance company. All kinds of craftspeople who worked in
the company could donate their handiwork to the sale, and proceeds
would go to benefit homeless kids."

My mind was spinning. *Wait, did you say all kinds of craftspeople who worked in insurance . . . would donate . . . to benefit homeless kids?*

"For the sale," he said, "I made a stained-glass panel, the kind you hang in a window. It was pretty large, about a foot wide by two feet high. It was a red rose in an arched panel with what they call a clear seedy background, clear with bubbles in it.

"One coworker was a single mom without much money. She would have liked to buy the panel, but she couldn't afford it. The rose panel was priced pretty high, and somebody else bought it. Twelve years later at her retirement ceremony, I gave her a red-rose panel I had made, just like the first one.

"Later she sent me the nicest thank-you note for it. She said she was touched by the fact that after twelve years I still remembered the rose glass panel she had loved."

Well, that just goes to show me. I shouldn't have judged a man by his business suit.

Like the insurance agent/stained-glass designer, Jesus was often prejudged by the people around him. Once he revealed his gifts and his messiahship, neighbors of Jesus kept asking, "Isn't this the carpenter?" (See Mark 6:1-6, NIV.) They simply couldn't believe that this humble carpenter was the great Messiah foretold in Scripture.

43

Sometimes people see us in certain categories: "Oh, he's an artist. He couldn't possibly know anything about cars." "She's blind, so why does she want to be a TV newscaster?" But God doesn't concentrate on our job or our outward appearance. God looks at the heart. ✤

BUILDING ON YOUR FAITH

Has someone ever prejudged you by the position you held in a company? What quick judgments do you tend to make when someone approaches you on the street? Why do you think we make these judgments? What do you think God sees when he looks at you?

PRAYER

Lord, as David says in Psalms, "Search me, O God, and know my heart" (Psalm 139:23, NLT). Root out any snap judgments I make about others, whether or not I mean to be critical. Let me be absolutely sure of your searching heart-love for me, so I can love others in that way.

HANDS-ON HELP

FRAME A RED ROSE IN GLASS. TO DRY THE ROSE, TIE STEM WITH STRING AND SUSPEND UPSIDE DOWN, AWAY FROM DIRECT SUNLIGHT AND DAMPNESS. TAKE THE BACKING OFF BOTH PHOTO FRAMES. SLIGHTLY PRESS THE DRIED ROSE BETWEEN THE TWO GLASS OVALS. INSERT IN THE SILVER FRAME. SCREW CUP HOOK INTO THE TOP OF A WINDOW FRAME AND ATTACH FISHING LINE. HANG FRAMED ROSE IN A WINDOW.

YOU'LL NEED:

ONE SILVER OR SILVER-TONED OVAL PHOTO FRAME WITH HANGING RING ON TOP

ONE INEXPENSIVE OVAL PHOTO FRAME, SAME SIZE AS ABOVE (YOU'LL USE JUST THE GLASS)

DRIED RED ROSE (SEE INSTRUCTIONS) WITH STEM CUT TO FIT INSIDE FRAME

FISHING LINE

CUP HOOK

A Constellation of Beads

*[God] decides the number of the stars and gives
each of them a name.*

PSALM 147:4, TJB

As anybody who knows me can tell you, my favorite color has always been blue. The bluer the better. One afternoon my younger son came in the door after school. "Here, Mom," he said, presenting me with a necklace of blue glass beads. They sparkled like a constellation of stars. There were beads of cobalt, turquoise, teal, and purplish blue.

"It's lovely," I said, turning it in my hands. Thinking he had just picked it up from the sidewalk, I asked, "Where did you find it?"

"I made it for you at school," he said.

"You made this? For me?! But why?"

He shrugged, smiling. "Because you like blue."

I took a deeper look at all the colors. "These cobalt glass beads are gorgeous," I said. "Where did they come from? Portugal?"

"Wait a minute; I know that one," he said, reaching for a world atlas and pointing to the first page. "I think those are from . . . Afghanistan."

"I see," I said. "And what about these greenish blue, diamond-shaped ones?"

"Those are from dinosaur eyes," he volunteered.

"And these purplish ones?"

"Oh, those are from melted atoms," he said.

"How do you know that?"

"The teacher told me."

"Are you sure you know where all these beads are from?" I asked him.

"Why do you want to know?"

"Because it's interesting."

"Well," he said slowly, "it's interesting if I make something up, too."

I can't argue with a creative mind. Like my son the necklace maker, God has an unfettered imagination. After all, God not only created millions of stars, but he also named each one. It's good to let our imaginations run wild so we can create things that are wildly beautiful and bold. ✤

BUILDING ON YOUR FAITH

The word *unfettered* implies taking off chains, setting free. Would you say that your imagination is fettered or unfettered? On a clear night, invite your family or a group of friends to find their own stars and name them. (It's interesting if they make something up.) What will you call yours?

47

PRAYER

Creative Father, you strung the stars like glass beads in the sky and named each one. As David wrote, "Such knowledge is too wonderful for me; it is high, I cannot attain unto it" (Psalm 139:6, KJV). I think you must love everything you've made, including me.

HANDS-ON HELP

STRING AN IMAGINATIVE NECKLACE OF GLASS BEADS. AT A CRAFT STORE GLASS BEADS ARE NORMALLY ORGANIZED BY COLOR. LOOK OVER THE WHOLE SELECTION OF YOUR FAVORITE COLOR, CHOOSING BEADS THAT STRIKE YOUR IMAGINATION. SO YOU WON'T HAVE TO WORRY ABOUT BUYING TOO MANY OR TOO FEW, YOU MIGHT WANT TO STRING THE BEADS AT THE STORE BEFORE PAYING FOR THEM. WORKERS THERE WILL PROBABLY BE GLAD TO HELP WITH CHOOSING STRING AND CLASPS, AS WELL AS WITH THE BEADING ITSELF.

YOU'LL NEED:

GLASS BEADS, MANY VARIATIONS OF ONE FAVORITE COLOR
STRING, CLASPS (AVAILABLE AT CRAFT STORE)

ROOM TO THINK

Her Grandmother's Apprentice

Hold tightly to the pattern of truth I taught you.

2 TIMOTHY 1:13, TLB

A long time ago (I believe it was in 1985), a young woman of Tlingit heritage named Rebecca came to show our Alaskan weaver's guild how she wove in the tradition of her tribe.

She sat on the living-room carpet, weaving a Tlingit blanket (a raven with a wild eye) and demonstrating how her grandmother taught her to weave in the Tlingit way on a vertical loom. "It's kind of a long process," she began in her dry, understated way of talking. "One blanket takes months to make. For one thing," she went on, "you need to dry the intestines of a mountain goat for the warp, because those are strong and pliable."

She let us feel some of the underbelly fur of a musk ox. "That's called *qiviut*," she explained. "It's the softest down, softer than goose down. If you can make a journey to the Arctic, try to collect some qiviut from the musk ox."

I tried to imagine collecting *anything* from a musk ox, much less its underbelly fur, without its express permission. "How hard would it be," I asked, "to collect the qiviut?"

Rebecca looked thoughtful for a moment, then smiled. "It's hard," she said. "You try to pick it up from the ground when they're not looking."

Rebecca turned back to her loom. "Weaving the same design that your elders made," she continued, "is an honor to them. It's a way of remembering their heart." As she worked wool through the warp with her fingers, she told us, "We Tlingits don't have the same kind of drive that most Americans do to make something different each time.

"Our way is to weave a blanket exactly the same from generation to generation. When I make it the way my grandmother taught me, I feel a flow that isn't cut off." Then she concluded stiffly, "But she's one of the last of the traditional weavers. And I am my grandmother's last apprentice."

That night I stomped home through the snow. *When Rebecca dies,* I thought angrily, *all the Tlingit blanket weavers will be gone.* I called my old friend, a storyteller who could almost be classified as a native himself, the way he speaks so eloquently with elemental words. He listened carefully to my story about Rebecca. "And she teaches others?" he asked.

"Well, yes," I said.

"Then when Rebecca is old," he soothed, "she will teach blanket weaving to her grandchildren."

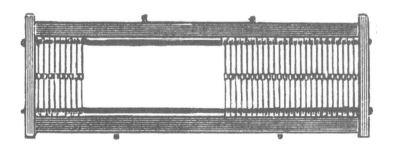

"And it will keep going?" I asked, like a child who knows the answer but needs to hear it spoken.

"Yes," he said, "I believe it will. It's the grandparents who keep a culture alive, by their stories and their faith and their craft."

Like Rebecca demonstrating her grandmother's way of blanket weaving, Jesus taught by patient example. He patterned his life after his Father, so his followers could learn from that example and pass it on. God has demonstrated his love to you through the interwoven love and faith of relatives and friends. ✤

BUILDING ON YOUR FAITH

How would your life be different if no one had taught you about Jesus through their stories and by example? Trace your "spiritual lineage" through family and close friends who have led you to a deeper understanding of God.

PRAYER

Lord, you have woven love through me. From generation to generation, through stories, crafts, and lessons of faith, my family and friends have passed on a spiritual legacy to me. Thank you for what they gave me. Show me how to continue that legacy with younger generations.

Hands-On Help

Weave a wall hanging with a child. For a "loom," notch the 8" plywood square at the top and bottom at 1/4" intervals. With garden string, wind a warp (lengthwise strands) around the top and bottom; tie off. Weave "found" materials from nature, such as pliable sticks, reeds, and grasses, through the warp. You can either leave your woven piece on the frame or cut it off in the center of the back. Tie fringe by taking a few strands at a time and knotting them together near the edge of the weaving.

You'll Need:

Scrap plywood, 8" x 8" x 1/4"
Waxed garden string
Materials found in
   nature

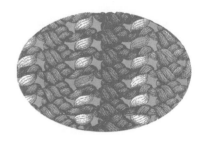

Braided for Love

*And we know that God causes everything to
work together for the good of those who love
God and are called according to his purpose
for them.*

ROMANS 8:28, NLT

My favorite shopkeeper, Rose, owned a secondhand store. It was
called—what else?—Secondhand Rose. She understood the whole
concept of a great secondhand store: buy rustic, handcrafted things,
sell them at a ridiculously low price, and keep customers happy by
being kind.

One day I stopped by the shop and saw a large rug braided in blues,
grays, and raspberry. It was rolled up on the pavement outside the shop.
I went inside and asked, "Rose, what's with the braided rug?"

"Just got it in from a little old lady who never stepped on it," she said.

"Oh, sure," I said.

"No, really. It's yours for a hundred and twenty-five."

"I'd give you a hundred, cash," I said.

"Sold."

"Wait!" I said. "Not so fast. Let me check the wear and tear."

As we walked outside together, she told me the history of the rug. "I just bought it from an elderly lady who made it for her husband while he was away in Europe in World War II. She made it from his old herringbone suit—see that black-and-white fabric there?—and she made it from her bright pink coat and from somebody's gray pants. But it's in perfect condition. Her husband died in the war, so he never got to see his present. As soon as she heard he'd died, she just rolled up the rug and put it away."

"That's been over forty years," I said, fingering the beautiful braids running flawlessly from color to color. "How did you happen to get it today?"

"Well," said Rose, "the lady called me this morning and said, 'I braided this rug for love. I can't keep it in my closet anymore. Somebody else needs it now.'"

I bought the braided rug. Now I wish I'd asked Rose for that elderly woman's name. It would have been a lovely thing to call to ask if I could visit her. Then I could have spread out the rug in her living room, exactly where she had planned to lay it when her husband came home from the war. She could have told me the origin of each piece of clothing. And I could have thanked her for the way she braided that rug for love.

Like the lady who braided the raspberry rug, God is braiding a beautiful work from the scraps of our lives: our times of wonder and discovery, times of grief, times of great joy. This can be comforting to know, especially when we're facing times of loss, when nothing seems to make sense in our lives.

What started as separate pieces now forms a striking pattern that spirals out from our birth and encompasses our every experience. One day, we'll see this "braided rug" in its entirety. We will be able to look back and see how God was in each moment of grief, each moment of joy, each questioning time. ✢

BUILDING ON YOUR FAITH

Think about some of the experiences that make up your life. What times made you wonder whether anything made sense? Have there been times when you wondered whether God was still working in your life? Can you see a loving pattern in the way God braided your own life experiences together?

PRAYER

Lord, sometimes I feel like my life is nothing but scraps. Nothing seems connected to anything else. Show me how all the scraps fit together into one piece. Then I can thank you for braiding the scraps together for love.

Hands-On Help

"Braid" a time line—actually a time spiral—of your life. With a pencil, draw a large spiral on watercolor paper. Starting from your birth in the center and spiraling out to the present time, label some important events, or "scraps," in the order that they happened. Label family births, deaths, important relationships, job transfers, and other life-changing experiences. Then apply a wash of watercolors: use a different color for each kind of experience, such as yellow for births, purple for job transfers. If you wish, date and sign your work, then add a frame.

You'll Need:

Dark pencil
Heavy watercolor
    paper
Watercolor paint
Picture frame
    (optional)

Finished Pieces

[God] has made everything beautiful in its time.

ECCLESIASTES 3:11, RSV

I once worked as a pottery painter in a studio/retail shop. All the pottery was brightly colored; on each piece we painted a wild animal.

One Saturday morning I brought my two sons to work with me so they could see how I spent my time. In the store window, I demonstrated pottery painting to customers and window-shoppers. For a while my sons watched me closely; then they disappeared.

After an hour I got up to stretch my legs. I found the boys in the workshop in back of the store. They were humming to themselves as they each painted a mug: a dolphin on one, a wolf on the other. When it was time to go home, we put away the mugs, and I told the boys I would bring the mugs home another day.

On Monday I came to work and painted bright backgrounds on the mugs: tropical blue water for the dolphin, purple sky for the wolf howling at the yellow moon. I brought the mugs home after they had been glazed and fired and placed them in a high kitchen cupboard, waiting for the right moment.

That afternoon the boys asked, "Mom, whatever happened to the mugs we painted?"

"I can't tell you where they are—," I began.

But they misunderstood what I was saying and groaned. "How could you lose them?" the firstborn reproached me. "Didn't you look in the shop where we put them so carefully?"

"Yes, but—"

The secondborn sniffed, "Mom, they're *endangered!*"

I smiled and patted his shoulder. "Oh, I'm sure they'll turn up."

That night after dinner, I fixed some hot cocoa and poured it into the new mugs. I placed the mugs on the table in front of the boys. With curious expressions, they stared at their own handcrafts.

"Cool," said the firstborn. "My dolphin."

"Wow!" the secondborn shouted. "I thought these were lost!"

"Not lost at all," I said. "They just weren't quite ready for you. Until today."

Like a pottery painter, God finishes his craftwork well. The outcome is better than we first imagined. Sometimes we create a dream of the way our lives could be. We imagine how we could best live and glorify God. For a while, though, our dream appears to be lost. We need to let some time pass. Maybe God is at work on our dream, completing it, making it beautiful in his good time. ❖

What are your big goals for your life? Do they all lead to the fulfilling of a specific dream or dreams? With those goals in mind, how much of your dream has been fulfilled? Do you feel that dream has been sidetracked or lost? Imagine God in his craft studio, working on your dream for you. In his hands, what could it become?

PRAYER

Lord, you are the author and completer of our faith. While you are busy completing our faith, that involves a lot of patience (or impatience) on our part. Make our good dreams take shape, so we can praise your work.

HANDS-ON HELP

PAINT A MUG. CHOOSE A MUG FROM A VARIETY OF PIECES AT A STUDIO. WORKERS THERE HELP YOU WITH PAINTING INSTRUCTIONS AND EQUIPMENT AT A VERY FAIR PRICE. WHEN YOU ARE FINISHED PAINTING, LEAVE YOUR MUG THERE AND PICK IT UP IN ABOUT A WEEK, ALL FIRED AND READY TO DRINK FROM. IF THERE IS NO POTTERY-PAINTING STUDIO IN YOUR AREA, CHECK YOUR COMMUNITY COLLEGE FOR POTTERY CLASSES.

YOU'LL NEED:

A DO-IT-YOURSELF POTTERY-PAINTING STUDIO IN YOUR AREA. (THESE KINDS OF STUDIOS ARE POPPING UP AROUND THE COUNTRY.) ALL EQUIPMENT IS PROVIDED AT THE STUDIO.

60

ROOM TO THINK

A Mosaic from Shards

*The Lord is close to the brokenhearted; he
rescues those who are crushed in spirit.*

PSALM 34:18, NLT

One Saturday on a tiny asphalt-covered island in New York
Harbor, I was feeling fragmented and lonely. I watched my young sons
climb the monkey bars at the playground, thinking about the boxes I
still had to unpack in the apartment. We had just moved there from
Palo Alto, California, a place of palm trees and fountains. I was missing something, but I couldn't name what it was. Though the island was
only a stone's throw from Manhattan, it had no bridges—only a ferry.
To me, it felt like Alcatraz.

While my sons were playing, I dug in the sand and came up with a
piece of blue-and-white pottery. I dug some more and found lavender,
white, and blue shards. The boys came over to watch. "What are you
finding?" they asked.

"Pieces of a puzzle," I told them. "These were plates and cups from
centuries of people who lived on Manhattan Island." I told the boys the
story of how our little island came to be made up almost entirely of
discarded ground from Manhattan. To make space for the web of subway

62

tunnels throughout New York City, workers carved out tons of rock, soil, and accumulated refuse. Then they dumped the ground just behind our small island, more than doubling its size.

"Come help me look for more pieces," I said. We dug like archaeologists, finding more pottery shards. We piled them all on a big rock.

"Now what do we do with all these pieces?" asked my practical son, the scientist.

"Make them go together," said my other practical son, the inventor.

"What should we glue them onto?" I asked.

"Well, we could put them around a picture frame," suggested the inventor.

So that evening we sat around the kitchen table, gluing the washed pottery around the border of a white wooden frame.

"It's like a puzzle, so it needs something to go inside the frame," decided the scientist.

The inventor searched the room. "I know!" From an open packing box, he grabbed what was on top: a blue-and-white ceramic sign. I hadn't remembered to hang it inside the new house. Fitting into the frame just right, the sign was the last piece to our puzzle. The sign said:

> Just to be
> with those we love
> is enough.

Maybe we feel fragmented, like tiny shards of pottery. But God can make a mosaic out of us. When we feel broken or shattered, we try to escape that feeling. Yet in that place, we might be on the verge of learning something new. Digging in our own ground, we find a treasure right under our feet. The very thing that seems bad—the brokenness— can be what brings us to a loving discovery. ✤

BUILDING ON YOUR FAITH

Think back to a time when you felt broken or fragmented. How did God help you through that time? Are you feeling fragmented in any part of your life right now? Meditate on Psalm 34:18, inserting your name in place of "the broken-hearted." Know that God is with you, no matter what the circum-stances are.

PRAYER

Lord, at times my heart has felt broken, and I have been crushed in spirit in a way only you can see. But I know you love me. Take my broken parts and make me into a loving mosaic.

HANDS-ON HELP

MAKE A MOSAIC FRAME FOR A CHILD'S ROOM. IF YOU DO NOT LIVE NEAR A RECYCLING STATION OR A BEACH, TRY DIGGING IN YOUR OWN BACKYARD AND SEE WHAT YOU COME UP WITH! OR BUY INTER- ESTINGLY SHAPED BEADS FROM A CRAFT STORE. ARRANGE PIECES AROUND A FRAME, THEN GLUE INTO PLACE.

YOU'LL NEED:

SMOOTH-EDGED POTTERY OR GLASS PIECES
    (FROM A RECYCLING
    STATION OR A BEACH)
WOODEN PICTURE FRAME
    SURROUNDING A
    FAVORITE MOTTO
GLUE GUN

Be Brave!

Yes, be bold and strong! Banish fear and doubt!
For remember, the Lord your God is with you
wherever you go.

JOSHUA 1:9, TLB

I used to tutor a first grader in art in my home. Allison and I never erased anything in our drawings. We called this "being brave." Instead of erasing, we incorporated the stray pencil mark into the drawing.

One day I gave her this poem:

Taking Art
For Allison, for later

In my house you can draw
a vegetable eating a boy
and spitting him out!
Close to your paper I can draw
one gray horse standing up
on two feet, dancing
with a pencil.

Once I heard a story
of a princess married to a poor
but wise artist. For years
the artist made the princess
work at art. He made her scrape
the fiddle, bake a kitchenful
of clay pots and slowly, slowly turn
brave, before he showed himself
to be a prince. Are you brave?

If you make mistakes, do you
erase? Or do you make a bumpy
line a cloud,
a gray slash mark a long cloud
of birds far away?

Since she was only seven, Allison could barely read this poem, much
less understand what I wanted to tell her. "You are such a great artist
already," I wanted her to know. "People will tell you you're making
mistakes, but you might just be 'working hard at art,' learning how to
become brave. People will correct your work, trying to shape it into something they're more comfortable with, because the unfamiliar scares them.

"Allison," I wanted to tell her, "be brave." But I knew it was too
much for her to handle at seven. That's why I wrote on top, *For Allison,
for later.*

That year Allison wrote and illustrated a story about a girl who
wanted magic ballet slippers. Her mother showed it to me and asked,

"Do you think it's any good?" All the illustrations were made from paper collage. They burst from the page like a ticker-tape parade.

"I wish I'd written it!" I said. "It's fantastic."

She hesitated for a moment. "There's an illustrated-book contest for schoolchildren in New York City . . ."

Shamelessly I fell on my knees and begged her to submit it. A month later, Allison knocked on my door and showed me her first-place medal. She looked like the princess who had slowly turned brave.

Like a brave artist, God doesn't erase things in me that others call "mistakes." I think he prefers to call them "character builders." He doesn't throw out my past pain or my new gray hairs. Instead, he incorporates everything into his overall design for my life. As Mother Teresa said, "Without mistakes, there is no forgiving. Without forgiving, there is no love." God has shaped our lives—warts and all—through his incomparable love. ✣

BUILDING ON YOUR FAITH

When you set down your own handcraft and stand back to view it for the first time, do you immediately try to take out the flaws? Resist the urge. This is good work that you have accomplished. What can you do to incorporate the "mistakes" into the overall design?

PRAYER

Lord, you are a brave artist. Somehow you are happy with the way I'm turning out. You see my flaws as part of your whole design. That's amazing to me.

HANDS-ON HELP

WITH A YOUNG FRIEND, MAKE COLLAGE SELF-PORTRAITS. COLLECT ABOUT EIGHT DIFFERENT COLORS OF CONSTRUCTION PAPER. TEAR IT INTO VARIOUS SMALL SHAPES. DON'T BE TOO CAREFUL ABOUT THIS. WITH THESE TORN SCRAPS, PIECE TOGETHER A SELF-PORTRAIT. USE A GLUE STICK TO ATTACH IT TO A PIECE OF BLACK CONSTRUCTION PAPER. NOW SIGN IT WITH A SILVER MARKER PEN AND HANG IT ON THE MIRROR IN YOUR BATHROOM UNDER THE WORDS: GOD SEES ME AS I AM AND LOVES ME. THAT'S BRAVE!

YOU'LL NEED:

EIGHT SHEETS OF
    DIFFERENT-COLORED
    CONSTRUCTION
    PAPER
GLUE STICK
SILVER MARKER PEN

A Hat Named Margaret

*Yahweh, you . . . know me . . . you read my
thoughts from far away.*

PSALM 139:1-2, TJB

One evening there was a knock at my door. When I opened it, my friend Katherine was there, smiling mysteriously, wearing her long blue shawl and a hat I hadn't seen before—black velvet with jewel-colored beads.

"Katherine!" I said. "Come in. What a great hat!"

She giggled. "Oh, good. I was hoping you'd notice. It's really yours, you know." She put it on my head, adjusting it. "There, the feather looks just right."

Katherine and I belong to a small arts group that meets every week. Along with our latest projects, we share food, prayer, news, and . . . well . . . clothes! After three years of meeting together, all of our closets now contain hand-me-downs from others in the group: belts, jackets, boots, and hats. And where did these clothes come from before our group started passing them around? From a secondhand store, of course. Who knows how many artists have worn Katherine's blue shawl? She has it now, but she will probably pass it on to someone else soon.

"Where did you find this great hat?" I asked, admiring it in the mirror. On one side was an intricately beaded floral design with a jaunty feather sticking out of the center.

"At a craft store," she said. "The hat was on a shelf, saying, 'I'm for Margaret.'"

"That's funny," I said. "I've never heard a hat talk."

Katherine nodded and went on. "I saw the hat and the beaded flower appliqué set side by side, and they were both saying, 'We're for Margaret.' So I picked them up. This afternoon I was sewing the appliqué onto the hat at the beach. A feather dropped on my beach blanket, and it said, 'Margaret,' too, so I stuck that in, and now it's yours."

"Thank you," I said with a grin. "It's perfect. Just today I was thinking I'd like to get a hat. You must have been reading my mind. But how did you know everything was saying 'Margaret'?"

Katherine opened the door to go out, turning to me with a swish of her shawl. "I just know you." She smiled.

Like my friend Katherine, the Holy Spirit sometimes arrives unannounced to drop a remarkable gift in our hands. What he brings is designed just for us. He knows our names, which reflect our inner natures. ✢

71

Have you ever crafted something with a certain friend in mind, then brought it to your friend's house as a surprise? What was the craftwork? What made you decide it should belong to that one friend? In what ways were the gift and your friend alike? Can you remember a time when God surprised you with a "handmade" gift just for you?

PRAYER

Lord, like a dear friend, you care about me so much. You even "read my thoughts from far away." You know what will make me smile. Thank you.

HANDS-ON HELP

MAKE A BEADED DESIGN ON A HAT. MANY CRAFT STORES HAVE BEADED APPLIQUÉS THAT ARE ALL READY TO SEW ONTO CLOTH. STITCH BEADED DESIGN TO SIDE OF HAT. ATTACH FEATHER.

YOU'LL NEED:

PLAIN BLACK VELVET HAT
BEADED FLORAL APPLIQUÉ (CHECK CRAFT STORE)
FEATHER

ROOM TO THINK

A Bed of Clouds

Meditate on God's wonders. . . . Whose skill details every cloud?

JOB 37:14; 38:37, TJB

One morning right after my sons left for school, I looked at my studio/guest room with a critical eye. Everything in the room was blue, teal, and white: the curtains, the pottery on the shelf, the glass bottles lining the windowsill. Everything, that is, except for one piece of furniture—the large guest bed in the middle of the room. The bed was a secondhand piece from the fifties and had a fake wood-grain, gray color that I think they used to call "pecan."

Something had to be done about that "pecan." It was ruining the whole creative ambiance of the place. First, I rifled through the storage closet for paint. All I could come up with was a gallon of white acrylic house paint and a set of food-coloring squeeze bottles. So I dumped some white paint in a coffee can. Then I dripped drops of blue and green food coloring into the can, hoping they would mix together. They did mix, but it took lots of drops to come up with a beautiful teal.

As I painted the bed, I was reminded of something the writer Opal

74

Whiteley said about the color blue. When Opal was only five or six years old, she kept a remarkable diary, where she talked about "the glad of blues":

> Morning is glad on the hills. The sky sings in blue tones. I do so like blue. It is glad everywhere. When I grow up I am going to write a book about the glad of blues.

I painted the whole bed. By early afternoon it had dried, but it didn't look quite finished yet. It needed something else. I had to think fast. The boys would come home from school in a couple of hours, and I wanted to surprise them with a finished art project.

I looked out the window for inspiration. In the sky floated enormous white cumulus clouds! I found a sponge, dipped it in the white paint and started dabbing lightly at the bed frame. Every cloud I made was a miniature of one I found outside my window.

Never before had I noticed how cleverly God crafts each cloud. Colors of the sky blended into the base of each cloud, and spongelike designs covered the white fluff at the top. I felt like I was a little child in God's art studio, creating not masterpiece clouds, but pretty good ones, using colors from his palette.

In no time, the bed was covered with clouds floating in "the glad of blues." When the boys came home from school, they surveyed the results. As usual, they

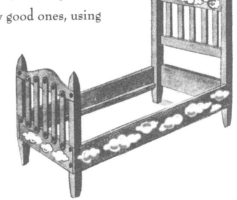

had differing opinions. One child stood back and frowned. Diplomatically he said, "Well, Mom, I guess that's the best you can do. So, I guess it's pretty good."

The other one yelled, "Cool! A cloud bed!" And with his finger he wrote his name in the still-wet clouds.

Like a painter, God handcrafts each cloud with a loving eye. As the book of Job says, his "skill details every cloud." When we study the clouds in the sky, we can see that nothing escapes the Creator's notice. God, the master painter, is in his art studio every day, working and playing. ✣

BUILDING ON YOUR FAITH

Do you ever look at the way God made the world and think he may have designed some things—like the parrot fish and the blue-footed booby—just for fun? Do you work playfully as well as carefully? Can you relax and make your craft more whimsical?

PRAYER

Master Designer, I can't believe how much fun you have with your creation. At the same time, your work is skilled and studied. If nothing escapes your notice, not even ephemeral clouds, then I know that nothing about my life will escape your notice. You created me, and you will not forget your creation.

Hands-On Help

Sponge-paint an old bed frame with clouds. Lightly sand bed frame. Pour one cup of white paint into pan. To achieve the color of sky you prefer, experiment by counting drops of blue and green food coloring into the pan. Note the number of drops of each color you use. Mix well in pan, then brush onto bed. Also brush a few broad sweeps of this color onto heavy white paper; set aside. Continue to use the same number of drops per cup of paint as you mix more paint as necessary. Let bed frame dry. Next, dip sponge in white paint, stamp off excess paint, and practice making different cloud formations on the heavy painted paper. (Hint: Use more paint on the bottoms of clouds, let more blue show through on the tops, and try for a loose pyramid shape.) Start sponge-painting the bed frame on less visible parts, then graduate to headboard.

You'll Need:

Old wooden bed frame that would be improved
   with a coat of paint
Sandpaper, brushes, roller pan
White semigloss house paint (1 or 2 quarts—
   save 1 cup for sponge-painting)
Blue and green food coloring (use green sparingly)
Round makeup sponge
Heavy white paper (or throwaway material)

Adorning a Story

A word fitly spoken is like apples of gold
in pictures of silver.

PROVERBS 25:11, KJV

Once I wrote a story I thought was fiction. What it meant, I had no idea. I just wrote it; I didn't understand it. When I met a new friend, I thought he might be able to understand it and explain its meaning to me, so I gave it to him. This is the whole story:

The Offering

Once there was a maiden who was so pure and strong that all the princes of the kingdom looked upon her with joy. The maiden was sad, though, and there was no one with whom she could share her heavy heart.

One day a poor man came from a far country. This man wept to see his friend so sad. (For already, at once, they were the best of friends!) "What is it?" he asked himself. "What is it that I can do for this poor soul? For I have nothing to offer her."

Then he remembered that he had a book in his pack. He brought it over to her, and he left it in her hand. As he left, he kissed her with all silence.

When the maiden opened the book, she found a garden and a pool of water with goldfish swimming, a cardinal beside the pool, a swing, a branch of holly berries, and a swan.

"Why did you give me this story?" my friend asked me.

"Because I thought you'd like it," I answered. "I wrote it a long time ago. I'm not sure if it means anything. If you get something out of it, let me know."

Not too long after, my friend and I met for lunch. "I have something for you," he told me. He took a small book from his backpack and gave it to me. It sat like a bird in my hands. Its cover was handmade paper mixed with tiny blue feathers. When I opened it, I found a postcard of a country garden. On the following pages I found a photograph of a goldfish, a magazine clipping of a cardinal over a pool, a card with holly berries, a cartoon of a little girl on a swing, and a sketch of a trumpeter swan in flight.

I paged through it again and again, laughing with amazement. My friend had entered my story and illustrated it, making his own gift from mine. "How could you make my story come to life like this?" I asked him.

He shrugged. "You wrote it."

"I told you I didn't have any idea what it meant," I reminded him.

"And what am I supposed to do with the rest of this beautiful book—all these blank pages?"

"Write another story." He smiled. "I'll find the artwork for it."

Just as my friend found pictures to illustrate my story, God lovingly "illustrates" our life stories in various ways. When you find yourself in a state of confusion, God may send a friend to help you see the situation more clearly. When you are wavering between two indistinct choices, he may lead you to a parable that helps you picture the situation and decide what to do. ✤

BUILDING ON YOUR FAITH

What are you experiencing right now that needs to be illustrated or clarified? When you were in confusing circumstances before, how did God "illustrate" that part of your life story for you?

PRAYER

Lord, sometimes I find it hard to understand the puzzling times I'm going through. Thank you for illustrating my life's story in loving and revealing ways.

HANDS-ON HELP

MAKE AN ILLUSTRATED BOOK FROM A BIBLE PASSAGE. TAKE A FAVORITE CHAPTER FROM THE BIBLE AND ILLUSTRATE IT WITH GREETING CARDS, MAGAZINE GRAPHICS, AND OTHER ARTWORK. INSTEAD OF LOOKING FOR HISTORICALLY ACCURATE ILLUSTRATIONS OF ANCIENT ISRAEL, CHOOSE ILLUSTRATIONS—EITHER SILLY OR WISE—THAT SHOW HOW THE PASSAGE WORKS IN TODAY'S WORLD. IT'S BEST TO FIND YOUR ILLUSTRATIONS FIRST, THEN TO ARRANGE THEM ON ALL THE PAGES BEFORE GLUING THEM DOWN, AND FINALLY, TO WRITE THE VERSES NEXT TO THE ARTWORK. MAKE THIS A RAINY-DAY FAMILY PROJECT OR A SUNDAY SCHOOL ACTIVITY.

YOU'LL NEED:

BLANK BOOK WITH MEDIUM-WEIGHT PAPER,
ABOUT 8-1/2" X 11"
OLD MAGAZINES, GREETING
CARDS, CAST-OFF BOOKS
WITH ILLUSTRATIONS
GLUE STICK
BLACK, MEDIUM-TIPPED
MARKER PEN

Marbling from Chaos

> *In the beginning God created the heavens and the earth. Now the earth was a formless void, there was darkness over the deep, and God's spirit hovered over the water.*

GENESIS 1:1-2, TJB

One day my friend Greg was paging through a course catalog for adult classes at the community college. A nuclear physicist, he had always leaned toward the logical math and science courses in school. But now that he had turned forty, he wanted to do something eccentric, outside the circle of logic. He decided to take a workshop in paper marbling.

When he walked into the art room where the workshop was held, Greg told me, his first inclination was to turn on his heels and walk out. The art room in the old building was all white-painted brick, with high clerestory windows. The wooden art tables were paint spattered. The students looked like artists. He was afraid.

"Even though I love the look of marbled paper," he told me, "I feel like a klutz when it comes to actually making art. Where's the rule book?" he asked, half joking. "Where's the manual?" And when he saw the students with three rings in each ear, he thought, *These are all artists. I'm not an artist. I'm an impostor.*

But the teacher encouraged him to stay. Greg realized it was probably too late to get a refund, anyway, so he shrugged and sat down at a table, quite unhappy.

But Greg learned how to marble paper that day. It only took a few sheets of paper, a strange combination of liquids, and blind trust. "At first it looked like chaos swirling around in the pan without any pattern," he said. "But then I put the paper facedown on the surface of the solution. When I picked it up, chaos was transformed.

"It reminds me of a quote by Ella Wheeler Wilcox," he continued:

> The splendid discontent of God
> with Chaos made the world.

Like a paper-marbling artist, God the Father made the world from chaos and a "splendid discontent"—a burning urgency to make something brand-new by hand. These are the ingredients we need to begin a difficult work of ours. Surrendering control to God, we place our lives "facedown" in that swirling, formless void called fear. When we look at our lives afterward, we find a fortunate surprise: a pattern in God's creation. ✤

What causes "splendid discontent" in you, so that you feel driven to create something? Name the worst "chaos" in your life right now. Could that chaos actually be the secret ingredient in what you create?

PRAYER

God, you are an artist. You handcrafted a beautifully marbled world from what was once chaos. Knowing that you have the power to create the world gives me the confidence to trust you with my life. Give me the imagination to see the chaos in my life as raw material for creativity.

HANDS-ON HELP

MAKE "MARBLED" GREETING CARDS. SINCE THE INSTRUCTIONS FOR PAPER MARBLING ARE LENGTHY, HERE IS AN IMAGINATIVE ALTERNATIVE. PLACE A PAPER TOWEL IN A PAN TO ABSORB WATERCOLOR SPATTERS. THEN UNFOLD ONE BLANK GREETING CARD AND PLACE THE INSIDE OF THE CARD FACEDOWN IN CAKE PAN. BRUSH ONE OR TWO QUICK, JAGGED LINES OF WATERCOLOR DIAGONALLY ACROSS THE OUTSIDE OF THE CARD, APPROXIMATING A MARBLE VEIN. DROP A MARBLE INTO THE PAN AND ROLL IT AROUND ON THE CARD, LETTING A PATTERN DEVELOP. LET DRY. REPEAT WITH ANOTHER COLOR AND ANOTHER MARBLE UNTIL YOU ACHIEVE THE DESIRED RESULTS.

YOU'LL NEED:

BLANK GREETING CARDS, MEDIUM OR HEAVY STOCK
  (STATIONERY/CARD STORE)
CAKE PAN OR SIMILAR PAN, 8" SQUARE
PAPER TOWELS
MARBLES
WATERCOLOR PAINTS AND BRUSH

ROOM TO THINK

Life Masks

> *If any one is in Christ, [that person] is a new creation; the old has passed away, behold, the new has come.*
>
> 2 CORINTHIANS 5:17, RSV

One year my friend Heidi invited a crowd of close friends to her house for a life-mask-making party. I should have known it was going to be interesting—and bewildering—when I read on the invitation "Bring your own facial materials." I brought eyeliner, blush, and lipstick to give my life mask some life.

The party was a frightening experience, the way good art is frightening when first encountered. "Split into groups of two," Heidi commanded. "Now, one from each group lie down on the tarps."

Half of us lay down in the living room while the other half bathed our faces with petroleum jelly—an unsettling sensation. My partner Nadine was, fortunately for me, a beautician skilled in applying facial masks made from mud or mashed avocado. She had no qualms about this kind of thing. But still, I felt desperately trapped, like a person about to be buried alive.

Nylon stocking over the hair. Plastic wrap over most of the face. Then the bandages of plaster.

I started talking fast, letting Nadine know where my safe-deposit box was stored. "It's got my will in there," I said. "Tell my family I love them. Ask Heidi if she'll make that nice chocolate cheesecake for the reception after my funeral."

There wasn't much time. Nadine was pulling out bandages from a bowl of wet plaster and molding them to my face. She snipped them close to the hairline, next to my ears.

"I can't see," I said. "It's dark in here. Are you sure you know what you're—"

Nadine stuck a straw in my mouth. "Breathe through that," she said.

I shut up. For a while everything was quiet. The mask makers were busy smoothing wrinkles from our plastered faces. I breathed through the straw. *Maybe this is what it's like to drown,* I thought. And I fell asleep.

When I woke up, the air was hot and roaring. I tried to open my eyes, but my flesh wouldn't cooperate. And that sound—where had I heard it before? At the hairdresser's? It was, I finally realized, the sound of a blow-dryer.

The noise stopped. Then I felt soft fingers at my cheeks, peeling away the dead white skin of my mask. Nadine laughed when I squinted in the sudden light. "Here," she said, handing me the hardened mask. "Take a look at yourself."

I held out the mask at arm's length. Nadine had done a good job of molding. The mask looked like me, I guess. But it was just a shell, with none of my spirit in it. "I look dead," I told her.

"Well." She grinned. "That's just your mask. You're very much alive."

That was a big relief to hear.

Just as Nadine helped me through the "trauma" of mask making, God lovingly leads us through the most terrifying experiences of our lives. He has no qualms about anything we're about to go through, because he's been there before. Knowing that, we can relax and let him lead us and work on us.

As we grow in Christ, he keeps peeling off layers of our old self. He takes off an outer layer, revealing more of our inside self. Each time that happens, we can take a look at the lifeless mask we are leaving behind. We are more alive now, like "new creations." ✜

BUILDING ON YOUR FAITH

How do you feel after you've taken off a constricting mask? When you are going through a terrifying experience, is it hard to trust someone else? During those times, why is it hard to trust God? After those frightening episodes are over, how do you feel about the trust-worthiness of God?

PRAYER

Lord, you know I don't want to go through terrifying experiences. But you know what you're doing. Do whatever it takes to "perfect my faith" until I can trust you utterly.

HANDS-ON HELP

MAKE PERSONALIZED MASKS WITH FRIENDS. THIS KIND OF MASK MAKING IS MUCH EASIER THAN PLASTER MOLDS. GATHER EVERYONE AROUND A TABLE PILED WITH PAINTS, PLAIN WHITE MASKS, AND DECORATING PARAPHERNALIA. HAVE YOUR FRIENDS PAINT THEIR MASKS ANY WAY THEY WISH. AFTERWARD, TAKE INSTANT PICTURES OF THE MASKED GROUP. YOU MAY FIND THAT MANY HAVE PAINTED THEIR MASK TO REVEAL THE WAY THEY SEE THEMSELF: CLOWNISH, ANGRY, SHY, LOVELY, AND SO ON.

YOU'LL NEED:

PLAIN WHITE PLASTIC MASKS
   (CRAFT STORE)
BRIGHT ACRYLIC PAINTS,
   INCLUDING SILVER AND GOLD
GLITTER, FEATHERS, SEQUINS,
   AND OTHER ADORNMENTS
GLUE

A Lesson in Terrazzo

*Whatever you do, work at it with all your
heart, as working for the Lord, not for men.*

COLOSSIANS 3:23, NIV

One day my friend Karen the artist called me up. "Hey, you want to
help me with a mural for a new downtown restaurant?" she asked. "The
owners want us to make a couple of five-foot palm trees in terrazzo."

"Sure," I said. "Just one question. What's terrazzo?"

"It's a mosaic of broken ceramic tiles. It's easy. I'll teach you.
Anyway, the owners, who call themselves The Two Bobs, are only able
to pay us a little bit. So they're not expecting us to make exquisite
Byzantine mosaics."

I keep forgetting one important thing about working with Karen.
Whenever she gets into a project, no matter how low paying, she forgets
about sleeping and eating. She works at the project with all her might.
We spent more than a week just preparing for the project: sketching palm
trees, choosing tile colors, and breaking up the tiles into mosaic pieces.

Night and day, whenever possible, we worked on those murals. Karen
put herself in charge of laboriously sanding the tile pieces by hand. She
taught me the more exciting job of arranging the pieces inside the chalk

outline she had drawn on the wall. A patient teacher, she let me figure out how to make them fit together like a puzzle.

But I was seething inside as I considered the slow progress of our monstrous mural project. What had started out as a minimum-wage job had turned into volunteer work, then progressively seemed like slave labor.

As the weeks turned into more than a month, however, I found myself growing content to work for hours on the mural. The palm trees reminded me of some coconut palms I had once rested under, next to a lighthouse in Florida.

"Are you happy?" Karen asked me one evening as we worked.

"I am," I told her. "Before, I was frustrated with this huge amount of work for such little pay; but now, I'm happy. I wonder how that happened."

"You're working hard at something you like," she answered.

She was right. I began to see that the mosaics were making visitors happy. Whenever carpenters and painters came in for the first time, The Two Bobs would proudly show off the crescent-shaped palm trunks rising into unfinished branches. "Beautiful job!" people would tell us.

I was beginning to learn the truth of what Mother Teresa wrote in *A Gift for God:* "There is always the danger that we may just do the work for the sake of the work. This is where the respect and the love and the devotion come in—that we do it for God, for Christ, and that's why we try to do it as beauti- fully as possible."

"Forget the pay," I told

Karen one night as we were leaving the restaurant. "I would do this for nothing."

But The Two Bobs had other ideas. First, they paid us our wages. Then they surprised us by installing a brass plaque inscribed with our names and an overly complimentary French title: *Les Artistes*. And now, every time we come to the newly opened restaurant, they welcome us with hugs, ask us to order anything on the menu, and when we are finished, they hand us our bill.

"No charge," it usually says. "Thanks again."

Like my friend Karen the *artiste*, the Holy Spirit is the best kind of teacher, working alongside us, encouraging our progress. As we work hard at what we love, we gradually lose track of how much others owe us for our labor. That is when we can find our work rewarding in deeper ways. As Mother Teresa said, "We do it for God . . . and that is why we try to do it as beautifully as possible." ✢

BUILDING ON YOUR FAITH

Recall a time when the hard, painstaking work of crafting something by hand became a pleasure for you. What made the difference? What did you learn, besides the craft itself? How is it that some people gain so little money for all their incredible efforts yet stay so happy?

PRAYER

Holy Spirit, Teacher, thank you for patiently leading me through a process, from grumbling protests to quiet happiness in my craftwork. And thank you for those who have done the same for me. Take this work as a gift of love to you.

Hands-On Help

Make a terrazzo mural of a tree. Start with a chalk outline of a tree on a bulletin board. Crack tiles into "terrazzo" pieces as follows: Place each tile inside rag. With your fingers, find the center of tile in rag; rap once with a hammer. Sand the sharp edges of each piece. Before grouting the tiles, practice making a layout by arranging terrazzo pieces within the outline. Spread the grout like peanut butter on a small part of the bulletin board and on the back of each tile piece. Press the tile firmly into place. Finish by filling in the spaces with grout. Clean grout off tiles with a wet rag.

You'll Need:

Bulletin board with wood frame
Inexpensive standard-sized
   ceramic tiles
   (light brown, sky blue, ocean
   blue, sand, white, three
   colors of green)
Rag, hammer, chalk
Ceramic tile sanding block
   (heavy-duty grit)
Ceramic tile grout
Small plastic grout spreader

93

Beach-Glass Jewels

When [you] . . . [find] happiness in [your] work,
this is a gift from God.

ECCLESIASTES 3:13, TJB

Patricia is a professional beachcomber, the only one I know. And I might as well say it: I am jealous of her. As part of her freelance job, she collects sand-washed glass from beaches and makes jewelry from things that most beachgoers step right over.

I bought some earrings from her market stall while visiting the Olympic Peninsula several years ago. Last summer I bought a bracelet from her at a Sunday fair in Seattle. Looking over the blue, green, rose, and lavender jewelry, I asked her how she got into the business.

She was direct about it. "I've always thought that we should do what we love."

"That's a great philosophy," I said. "And I live by that, too. But sometimes it's hard to get paid for doing what you love."

Patricia talked as she wrapped some globes of rose glass with silver wire. "I love the peace and serenity of wandering the beaches. As Thoreau said, 'My life is like a stroll upon the beach, as near to the ocean's edge as I can go.' I agree with him. For me, it all started a few years ago with the very crazy idea that I could collect beach glass for a living. I decided to commit myself to spending as much time as I could in that enterprise."

"A beach-glass enterprise," I repeated. "I like that. And it seems to be working for you!"

She smiled and spread her arms out, encircling the beach-glass jewelry on the market table. "It's true," she said. "I enjoy my work. Every day I'm finding a purpose for glass that always wanted to be loved. Who would have ever guessed that all these little jewels once came from old throw-away bottles?"

Like the beachcomber, God the Creator finds great happiness in his work. He "combs" the world every day, searching for those of us who have been pummeled by harsh forces. Jesus said, "I, the Son of Man, have come to seek and save those . . . who are lost" (Luke 19:10, NLT). God brings us to his workshop and gives each of us a shining purpose. In his hands we become jewels. ✢

What has given you the greatest sense of purpose in your life? When do you feel great happiness in your work? Does your work give you both happiness and purpose? If not, what do you think is missing? Where can you find what you're looking for?

PRAYER

Lord, I was once lost, but you found me. Hold me in your hand like a jewel, and bring me to your workshop. Give me a loving purpose in all that I do today.

HANDS-ON HELP

MAKE EARRINGS FROM BEACH GLASS. WRAP EACH STONE IN SILVER OR GOLD JEWELRY WIRE, AS IF WRAPPING A PRESENT WITH RIBBON. LEAVE 1/4" OF THE WIRE UNWRAPPED TO ATTACH IT TO EARRING PARTS WITH PLIERS. (IF UNSURE HOW TO DO THIS, ASK AT CRAFT STORE.)

YOU'LL NEED:

TWO PIECES OF SMOOTH BEACH GLASS, ALMOST IDENTICAL
   (OR TWO SMALL, SEMIPRECIOUS STONES LIKE TURQUOISE
   OR TIGER'S EYE)
THIN JEWELRY WIRE (CHECK CRAFT STORE)
EARRING PARTS (CRAFT STORE)
NEEDLE-NOSE PLIERS

ROOM TO THINK

Tigers!

[Jesus] came to a village where a woman . . .
welcomed [him] into her home. . . . Mary sat
on the floor, listening to Jesus as he talked.

LUKE 10:38-39, TLB

A few summers ago my housemate, Adrienne, invited her friend "Grandfather Misha" from Siberia over for dessert. Adrienne was always inviting visitors from Russia to the house.

But Misha wasn't just any visitor. He was ninety-three years old and blind in one eye. During the Russian Revolution, Misha was already a teenager! He had once been a great hunter in his village. I sensed there was something holy about him.

That night as we ate, Misha told us about the gray Siberian tiger that came near a Russian village and about the hunters who pursued it to protect the village. He looked intently at me while he told the story in Russian, without waiting for Adrienne to translate, so she had to talk low under his beautiful voice.

He sounded like a young child as he told the story, almost singing. As a character in Amy Tan's *The Joy Luck Club* says: "Now that I am old, moving every year closer to the end of my life, I also feel closer to the beginning."

I was transfixed. This was a story about himself, I surmised. When the hunters tried to kill the tiger, said Misha, it attacked one hunter. It grabbed his arm and slashed his eye; then it walked away. It did not kill him. So the hunter stopped chasing the gray tiger that day and did not hunt anymore.

Adrienne turned to me and said, "That's like the clay tiger you made when you were little." I nodded. When I was six, I had loved tigers more than any other animal. I even had tiger dreams. Because I had only gray modeling clay at the time, I could only make a gray tiger. Some things get lost overnight, but some go with you everywhere you move. Through twenty moves I had held onto this gray tiger; that's why Adrienne knew about it.

In the kitchen she told me, "When people in Misha's hometown ask him deep questions, he answers quickly in a few words by telling a story. But since he's so old, the stories are the same few, over and over. So you can't really take them as advice for your own life." *Maybe not,* I said to myself; *maybe so.*

After dessert Grandfather Misha embraced me, Russian style. Then he said something over and over, intently. I thought he was saying, "Thank you for the dessert; it was delicious, thank you." But Adrienne was listening. "Don't forget,' he says. 'Don't forget!'" It was a message for me.

No more language was needed. He went out the door. How could he know that, more than anything else, I wanted to remember that night?

To hold onto the stories, like a fading dream. I ran outside. "Wait!" I called to him. He stood in the road, waiting. I ran upstairs, grabbed something off my curio shelf, and met him outside. "Don't forget," I said, handing him the clay tiger I had made.

He bowed low. "Don't for-get," he said carefully in English.

Under Grandfather Misha's intense gaze, I felt the way Mary might have felt when she sat at the feet of Jesus. Like Jesus, Misha spoke in a simple language that cut to the heart. When he looked at me so intently, I could almost understand what he was saying without translation.

"The wise know nothing," the poet Ikkyu said, "except maybe one song." Maybe that's all they need to know. For me, Misha's song was "Don't forget." I gave him the clay tiger so he wouldn't forget me. ✤

BUILDING ON YOUR FAITH

When did you last sit and listen to a wise person? What do you remember from that time together? Think about giving this person something you have handcrafted. How can you present it as a symbol of friendship and remembering?

PRAYER

Lord, as the wise Lakota man Black Elk prayed to you, "Grandfather, you have made the good road and the hard road to cross. And where they meet is a holy place." Thank you for those holy times we share with wise friends.

Hands-On Help

Make clay tigers with a very young friend. Shape clay into tigers. Press tiger's-eye stones in eye holes. You can find these stones at a shop that specializes in rocks. Allow to harden; paint stripes. As you make the tigers, tell a story about a tiger together.

You'll Need:

Self-hardening clay
Acrylic paints and brushes
Tiny tiger's-eye stones,
    2 per tiger (check
    rock shop)

Windows to the Heart

*The invisible attributes of God . . . have
been plainly discernible through things
which he has made.*

ROMANS 1:20, PHILLIPS

When I walked into the house of Isabel, a folk-art painter, I felt I had
just stepped through a threshold, nothing more, and stepped right out
the back door again. For there in her three hundred-year-old Vermont
farmhouse was a pastoral scene painted all over her walls. Stretched out
before me were rolling fields, creeks, and fences. Here and there I saw
a house and a barn. It was just like the view around her own farm.

"Come on in and look around if you feel like it," said Isabel. "I've got
some coffee on." I walked from one pastoral scene into another. The
whole house was like one big painting, every wall like a window, showing
another view of the fields outside.

While we sipped coffee in the parlor, I asked her, "What made you
turn your house walls inside out, so they show what's outside?"

"There's one difference between outside and inside these walls," she
said. "See if you can find it."

I looked out one window and compared the outdoor scene to the

p3

p4

p5

p6

p7

p8

p9

p10

mural on that wall to see if Isabel had actually painted the same view. It *was* the same, except for one thing: a red barn and a white farmhouse appeared in the mural but not in the actual view.

"Whose farm is this?" I asked.

Isabel stood close to the mural as if peeking in the farmhouse windows. "That's my husband's old place," she said. "It's where he grew up in Maine."

I turned to another wall, spotting another farmhouse. This one was a yellow Victorian with a yard full of chickens. "And whose is this?"

"Oh, that?" She cracked a smile. "That's where I grew up. It's down the road about twenty miles."

On another wall was a group of odd-sized shacks huddled together, leaning on one another. "That's in Baltimore, where we lived during the depression," she said, "my parents and me."

"Is every house on this landscape a special place for you and your family?" I wondered.

"Oh yes," she said. "It's a way of rememberin', I suppose. Most people can't see what their own heart sees."

Isabel painted old places of family significance into the heart of the present. The murals show the truth behind what the eye sees. Like this painter, God sees inside each of our lives and makes invisible things visible. Things of the heart are there in plain view for those who share the heart of God. ✤

BUILDING ON YOUR FAITH

What attributes do you see in yourself that could be hidden from a casual observer's eye? Can anyone else understand what you've gone through in your life? How would you paint a mural of your heart life?

PRAYER

Lord, you can see through my exterior to what is invisible to others, my great and painful past and present. I cherish each experience because it's all part of the landscape you are painting of my heart life.

HANDS-ON HELP

STENCIL A PERSONALIZED FOLK-ART BORDER. CHOOSE A COMBINATION FROM THE STENCILS THAT SYMBOLIZE A PART OF YOUR INNER LIFE, SUCH AS A TULIP, A CAT, AND AN OPEN BOOK (SYMBOLIZING YOUR LOVE OF BEAUTIFUL, QUIET DAYS) OR A SEASHELL, A WAVE, AND A WHALE (SYMBOLIZING YOUR LOVE OF THE OCEAN). FOLLOWING DIRECTIONS ON THE STENCIL PACKAGE, ALTERNATE YOUR STENCILS IN A LINE AROUND THE ROOM. YOU CAN CHOOSE TO STENCIL AROUND WALLS JUST BELOW CEILING OR AT CHAIR-RAIL HEIGHT.

YOU'LL NEED:

A ROOM THAT COULD USE A STENCILED BORDER

STENCIL PAINT (CHOOSE SOFTER FOLK-ART COLORS,
   IF DESIRED)

STENCILS (SEE INSTRUCTIONS)

STENCIL BRUSH OR MAKEUP SPONGE

Caitlin's Bracelet

*The favors of Yahweh are not all past, his
kindnesses are not exhausted; every morning
they are renewed; great is his faithfulness.*

LAMENTATIONS 3:22-23, TJB

One Monday night I walked over to my friend Ben's house to jam;
a few of us meet every week to play folk music. Fiddle, guitar, recorder,
harmonica, and mandolin—the instruments make happy sounds
together, though we rarely know the music before we play it. We impro-
vise, and that way we let surprises come.

When we were about to start playing, I saw Ben's young daughter
Caitlin, an aspiring author, come shyly into the dining room. I called her
over. "Come on," I said. "I don't bite." She crept over, smiling, sensing a
secret handoff.

"Close your eyes," I said. "Now hold out your hands." I placed a
book about a wood fairy atop her open hands. She opened her eyes and
gasped, "Dad, look! This is perfect! It's just what I need for the book
I'm writing!"

I showed her the illustrations of the fairy's house, which was so small
that a tiny scallop shell stood by the fireplace as a shovel for cinders. She

read the whole book in a few minutes, standing next to me at the dining table, while the group started with a folk song we all knew slightly.

"Now I have something for you," Caitlin whispered to me. "Hold out your hand." I stopped playing my guitar and dutifully held out my right hand. She tied a blue-and-yellow beaded bracelet around my wrist. It looked new and freshly made. "I won't make it too tight," she promised.

"Would you double knot it, please?" I asked. "I don't want to lose it." She did.

When Caitlin had gone upstairs to bed, I told Ben what his daughter had done for me. "I can't believe she just happened to have a fresh bracelet in her hand," I said. "As if she always carries around a present, in case anyone gives *her* one."

Ben laughed at the thought of it. "Sounds like something the whole world could do," he said.

Because Caitlin had a beaded bracelet ready in her hand, she was open to receive and give in return. Like young Caitlin, God the Creator delights in giving away what he makes. From ruby pomegranates to crystal frost, God offers the world his jewel-like creations a trillion times a day. Since God is so generous with his craftwork, we can trust we'll never be empty-handed. We can freely give away the fruit of our gifts and talents to others. ❖

107

Have you ever given away a treasure and immediately received an unexpected gift in return? How did you react to the surprise? How has God shown his open-handed kindness to you in the past few days?

PRAYER

God, giver of all good things, thank you for your kindnesses to me. I can't outgive you. I see your love in the surprising gifts I've received from others.

HANDS-ON HELP

MAKE A BEADED BRACELET FOR A YOUNG FRIEND. KNOT ONE END OF THE STRING. YOU CAN STRING BEADS REPEATEDLY IN THE FOLLOWING ORDER UNTIL BRACELET IS THE SIZE YOU WANT: ONE LARGE RED BEAD, TWO SMALL BLUE ONES. KNOT THE ENDS TOGETHER AND SNIP OFF EXTRA STRING. YOU MIGHT WANT TO KEEP THIS PRESENT WITH YOU UNTIL AN UNEXPECTED MOMENT WHEN YOUR FRIEND COULD USE A SURPRISE LOVE GIFT.

YOU'LL NEED:

TRANSPARENT "JEWEL" BEADS: LARGE RED, SMALL BLUE (OR YOUR CHOICE OF COLORS)

THIN LEATHER STRING OR SIX-STRAND EMBROIDERY THREAD, ABOUT 4" LONGER THAN WRIST MEASUREMENT

ROOM TO THINK

The "3" Sign

*And if, as my representatives, you give even a
cup of cold water to a little child, you will surely
be rewarded.*

MATTHEW 10:42, TLB

Every day after school, neighborhood children run to my friend
Nancy's house. They sit at her kitchen table, draw horses, drink juice,
and eat carrots; she welcomes them.

Nancy told me about a few presents she'd made for her next-door
neighbor Jacob, whom she calls "The Noticer." He notices everything
around him and loves to point out anything new. When Jacob was
one year old one fall day, Nancy made a bright, smiling pumpkin face
out of construction paper and taped it in a small, high closet window
that faced his bedroom window. He liked it so much he named it
"Punky."

On the night before his second birthday, which was a big deal for
him, Nancy painted a giant multicolored *2* on white cardboard and
propped that in her window facing Jacob's. On his birthday morning,
Jacob looked outside to see that *2*. When his parents told him Nancy
made it because he had turned two, his face lit up.

Nancy knew that her third window-surprise sign for Jacob needed to be more dazzling than the first two, since he was developing sophisticated tastes. Still, the project had to be quick, homegrown, and not too expensive. "I found some gold Christmas lights in a box," she said, "and the next thing I knew, I was punching holes into cardboard and poking those lightbulbs through the holes."

As it turned out, these bulbs were the very exciting flashing-light variety. Nancy hung the sign in her window, plugged it in, and waited. That evening Jacob had some young friends over for a birthday dinner. "I could hear the surprised screams through the walls." She grinned. "It's a cool thing to delight and amaze children with random acts of twinkle lights."

Nancy said to me, "This is what the sign says: '3.' This is what it says to him: 'Jacob is special.' What he understands from that is 'Nancy cares.'"

The next day around sunset, Nancy lit the sign again for Jacob, and every day at sunset for two months, she plugged it in so he could see it glowing. "Just before I went on vacation," she said, "I went to his house and gave him the sign to keep. When I got back from vacation, I looked out my bedroom window. There it was, all lit up in his window facing mine."

Like Nancy, Jesus welcomed children into his circle of friends. He shows God's empathy to those who feel small in the eyes of the world. Jesus "shines a light" for us, reminding us that he really cares about each one of us. We are valuable to him. We can show our thanks by reflecting that light back to him. ❖

BUILDING ON YOUR FAITH

Think of a time when you were young and someone gave you "a cup of cold water" as a token of love. Do you remember how you felt when that happened? Name some things that Jesus said in the Gospels to show that he truly cared about people.

PRAYER

Light of the World, sometimes I just want you to make a special lighted sign for me and hang it where I can see it from my bedroom window. Would you please show me a personalized sign that you love me, that you care, that I'm valuable to you?

HANDS-ON HELP

MAKE A SIGN FOR A NORMALLY FORGOTTEN NEIGHBOR. WITH A MARKER PEN, DRAW A LARGE NUMERAL OR USE WORDS TO CREATE A MORE ELABORATE SIGN. WITH AN ICE PICK, MAKE HOLES ALONG THE OUTLINE OF THE LETTERING. INTO EACH HOLE, PLACE ONE CHRISTMAS BULB. IF THERE ARE ENOUGH EXTRA LIGHTS ON THE CORD, TAPE THEM ALL AROUND THE CARDBOARD TO MAKE A LIT FRAME. HANG IN YOUR WINDOW, FACING YOUR NEIGHBOR'S HOUSE.

YOU'LL NEED:

LARGE MARKER PEN
CORRUGATED CARDBOARD, ANY SIZE
ICE PICK
SMALL WHITE OR GOLD CHRISTMAS LIGHTS

A Symbol of Birds

As birds flying, so will the Lord of hosts defend
Jerusalem; . . . he will deliver it, and passing over
he will preserve it.

ISAIAH 31:5, KJV

Last summer, a few hours after my sons had flown from Seattle to see their dad at his house across the country, Nadia came to visit. She is from an old village in Russia and understands many things that we Americans tend to overlook—things of the soul.

Nadia knew that the boys had left for a long time. In the back garden under the apple trees, we sat eating a summer dinner. Nadia studied me, concerned. "How are you?" she asked me in English. It was brave for her to speak our strange language aloud.

"Fine," I said. "No, actually I am sad today."

Nadia looked unsurprised and said, "Yes."

For a while, we let the time go by without us. Then she asked, "What did you learn today?"

"You knew I would learn something?" I asked.

"Of course." She smiled. "We say in Russia: 'Every day is a messenger from God.'"

"Well, there were two wild geese," I began slowly, unsure how much English she would understand. She nodded quickly, as if to say, *Yes, yes, I know, two geese.* "When the plane took off," I continued, "I saw two geese fly up, right past the airport window. They were together, right next to one another. They looked strong."

"Yes," she said. "Those were your sons."

"Right," I said. "They were strong enough to fly across the country together."

"The geese have two homes," she said. "And they will come back here because you are their home as well."

"Yes, that's what I learned," I said. "After the plane left and the geese flew over, I walked outside the airport and looked down. There was a white feather at my feet. I picked it up. It was a goose-down feather."

"Down?" she asked. "What is goose down?"

"The softest feather," I answered. "The mother uses it for her nest."

"That is a very good sign," said Nadia.

Before she left that evening, Nadia handed me a small, black velvet purse with a woven strap in red and black and some Russian coins inside. On the front, in vivid fabric paint, was a strikingly powerful rooster. It had sharp spurs on its feet and a squirming mink in its mouth. "The rooster is

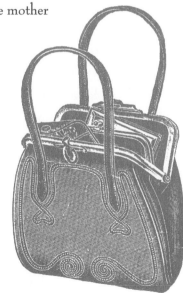

our sign for a child's soul," Nadia told me. "My daughter made the purse. She is twelve years old, like your son, the one with glasses. You take it now."

The rooster purse hangs on my bulletin board next to my favorite photograph of the boys. To me it is a good gift, a reminder that a child's soul is strong enough to fly across the country, powerful enough to overcome a terrible thing.

Like Nadia, God sees directly into our hearts and knows what we need. He surprises us with something just right: a gift God created. The gift is dear to him as well as to us. Nadia gave me a purse her daughter had made, and God gave me the gift of two wild geese. More powerful than just souvenirs of remembrance, gifts like these are symbols of God himself, loving and preserving us. They are tokens of his great affection and a promise of his deliverance. ❖

BUILDING ON YOUR FAITH

Recall a time when you were sad. How did a friend help you feel better during that time? Did he or she give you a gift? If the gift was handcrafted, why did that make it more valuable? What kind of gift can you offer to someone who is sad today?

PRAYER

Lord, you hover over me like a mother bird. I know you love me, because you keep reminding me in so many highly creative ways, through so many handmade symbols.

Hands-On Help

Paint a rooster on a purse. You can paint the rooster or any design you choose, even abstract dots and squiggles. Follow directions on the fabric-paint label. For the rooster, use red for the outline of its body; green for the tail feathers; orange for the comb; blue for the eyes, beak, and feet; and yellow for more feathers. Offer it to a friend as a symbol of God's careful and loving protection.

You'll Need:

Plain black fabric purse

Fabric paint (red, yellow, blue, green, orange)

Violet Soap

Stir up the gift of God, which is in thee.

2 TIMOTHY 1:6, KJV

Not long ago my friend and former English professor, Violet, called to say, "I want to treat you to lunch downtown today."

"But I don't have any money to pay you back," I said. "Unless you want to wait a few years when I'll be a famous and rich poet."

"Famous, yes," she laughed. "As for rich, well, I'd be surprised and happy for you."

When we met for lunch, she told me of a time in her life when she made fresh bars of soap for her family. She and her husband had no money for luxuries, with five kids to feed, clothe, and scrub. So Violet made the family's soap herself, saving scraps from odd pieces, heating them, and molding them together. She made the soap, not from a surplus of spare time, but out of a driving necessity.

Violet and I have been friends for almost twenty years. We met when I was a student in her college course Writing Creatively. Violet encouraged us to write with different colors of pens. "Find a color that makes you feel most creative," she advised. "Of course, I like violet, myself!"

Both kind and wise, she critiqued our work with the gentlest words. One semester, I invented an independent study course, just so she and I could discuss poetry. For a few hours in the winter weeks, we would hunch over her desk in her third-story office garret. There she showed me how to take scraps of my poems, heat them up with just-right words, and mold them together like fresh soap.

After our talk at the café the other day, I left a basket of violets and a batch of hand-molded soap by her office door. On a card I wrote the reason: "For all your gifts of Violet to me."

Like Violet, the Holy Spirit encourages us to use the resources around us creatively. Paul encouraged Timothy, "Stir up the gift of God, which is in [you]" (2 Timothy 1:6, KJV). Violet essentially said the same to her students in her admonition to "work creatively." Our gifts and talents are already inside us, put there by God. All we need to do is stir them in our hands and mold them into provisions for others. ❖

What gifts and talents do you feel are inside you, waiting to be stirred up? Who would benefit if you shared these gifts? How do you like to be encouraged? How do you encourage others to use the gifts of God?

PRAYER

Lord, thank you for the Holy Spirit who stirs up the gifts that are right inside me, and who sends others to stir up these gifts. Help me recognize the opportunities you provide, so I can use these gifts.

HANDS-ON HELP

MAKE SOAP BALLS FOR YOUR GUEST BATHROOM. PUT A SMALL HANDFUL OF SOAP SCRAPS IN A BOWL. RUN HOT TAP WATER OVER THEM UNTIL THEY SOFTEN LIKE CLAY. ROLL INTO BALL IN YOUR HANDS; ALLOW TO DRY.

YOU'LL NEED:

SCRAPS OF SOAP, SORTED BY COLOR OR MIXED TOGETHER
HOT TAP WATER
MEDIUM-SIZED BOWL

ROOM TO THINK